War Calls, Love Cries

A Civil War Novel by

Mark Barie

Barringer Publishing, Naples, Florida
www.barringerpublishing.com
Cover, graphics, layout design by Linda S. Duider

ISBN: 978-0-9989069-5-9

Library of Congress Cataloging-in-Publication Data
War Calls, Love Cries/Mark Barie
Printed in U.S.A.

This is a work of fiction. All characters, organizations, and events portrayed in this novel are either products of the author's imagination or are used fictitiously.

Dedication:

To my wife, Christine, for her assistance,

her support, and her love.

Acknowledgements:

My first attempt at publishing a novel would have failed miserably, were it not for the encouragement of family. For all those times I prattled on and on about matters trivial, and you were too polite to object, thank you! Thank you, Eric & Maggie, Oliver & Sierra, Alexandra & Eric, and Sebastian. I love you all.

P.S. Brace yourself.
There is another book
in the works.

Table of Contents:

Chapter 1

Dreams

The old man stopped in his tracks.

He clutched at his chest, eyes wide with fear and face contorted in pain. The farmer's milk bucket slipped from his hand and spilled its contents on the barn floor. He collapsed in a crumpled heap and gazed helplessly, as the warm, white river drained into the gutter at his feet. His vision of the barn's dirty and frozen interior faded into darkness.

The monstrous bull in the stall nearest the motionless figure on the floor lumbered toward his master. Although tethered by a thick rope through a ring in its nose, the animal placed its massive head between the wooden rails. Breath from the beast's nostrils created two, steaming jets, caressing the old man's head. The bull investigated further but only for a moment. He returned to his breakfast of corn husks and hay, leaving the old man to die in the subzero temperatures of that cold winter's morning.

Outside, in the barnyard, Isaac Wells worked with a sense of urgency as he forked hay into the pasture. The two old mares, although hungry for their meal, were not as anxious as the seventeen-year-old, who yearned for the warmth of the barn. Despite the frigid cold, Isaac stopped long enough to stroke each of his equine friends. Ice and snow crunched under the young man's feet as he walked the well-worn path to the ramshackle barn. The young man trudged up the slight hill, his chin buried in the collar of his coat, to avoid the sting of wind-driven snow. He smiled when his thoughts drifted to law school. Isaac, scheduled to graduate from the village school in May of next year, would begin his legal studies in the fall. The school in Albany, although founded just nine years ago, in 1851, enjoyed a good reputation. Isaac's replacement on the farm would be his brother, John. The older sibling, caught drinking on the job at Split Rock Mine not once but twice, did not have a choice. Still, John lied to the old man about why he lost his job, but Isaac said nothing, less his plans for law school be disrupted. The young man smiled despite his brother's deceitful ways because, within the year, Isaac would swap his pitchfork for a pencil.

The boy's comforting thoughts were interrupted when Isaac fought with the barn door. Forced to scrape several inches of freshly fallen snow, he pushed and pulled on the on the rusted handle with all his weight. After a few minutes and several failed attempts, his muscular arms produced an opening just wide enough for the boy to squeeze through.

"Father, I fed the horses and the pigs. I can help you with the rest of the . . ."

Isaac stopped in mid-sentence.

"Father?"

Isaac found the old man's face cold to the touch, the boy cursing the winter wind that whistled through the barn. Thoughts of his dying father triggered memories of his dead mother. Emma died a slow and painful death, just five years ago. She suffered greatly, and so did her family. Isaac could not bear the thought of losing his father too. He forced himself to concentrate on the effort required to move one hundred and sixty pounds of dead weight from the barn to their farmhouse. The one-story wood frame structure, the only home Isaac ever knew, looked old and dilapidated, with large sections of clapboard now missing. Mother Nature filled the mostly curtain-less windows with cobwebs and dead flies, something Mother Emma strictly prohibited.

Isaac struggled as he carried his father to the house. The young man grunted as he climbed the three steps onto the large porch that surrounded two sides of the home. The porch, covered with dirt, old furniture, and windblown snow, stood as a poor tribute to the memory of that woman who truly believed that cleanliness was next to godliness. As Isaac approached the door, his father's dangling feet sent an abandoned rocking chair into a vigorous back and forth motion. It banged against the wall of the house and shed some of its snow, in protest. The rocking chair moved as it did in the past when Abraham Wells leapt to his feet in response to Emma's screams. But abandoning his wood and wicker perch did nothing to ease the pain which racked her body. The consumption from which she suffered did not yield. When she died, she took with her the hearts of two men and the love of a twelve-year-old boy. The husband she left behind lost his way and struggled with loneliness, almost daily. The eldest son, angry and bitter, sought solace in a bottle. However, her youngest boy seemed to draw strength from his mother's passing, his determination fierce, his focus laser like. Nothing would stop him.

And yet, on this cold and blustery morning, Isaac thought about stopping. He thought about giving up. His heart ached for the old man. His eyes burned with tears of fear, and the muscles in his arms screamed for relief. The devoted son refused to rest until he placed his father on the torn and worn Victorian sofa in the parlor. The decrepit piece of furniture, once his mother's pride and joy, now cradled the man she regularly embraced long ago.

The boy shed his hat and coat, revealing a sweat-soaked shirt and golden locks dusted with snow and melting ice. He wiped his brow with shirt sleeves too snug for his thick arms and inhaled deeply to catch his breath. He stared at the old man, not knowing what he should do next.

His eyes grew wide when he focused on the farmer's pained expression. Perhaps he imagined things, but his father's sickly gray color changed. The agony on Abraham's face slowly transformed itself into peaceful exhaustion. Maybe, an old piece of furniture could heal the sick and the dying. Isaac dropped to his knees, but not in prayer. He pressed his ear to the man's chest, desperately hoping for some sign of life. And then he heard it–the faint beats of a weakened heart.

Fiona Dunham took the plate of cornbread muffins from the dining room servant at the Ausable House and thanked the gray-haired Negro with a forced smile.

She knew from experience that the muffins were at least two days old but covered them anyway with a red, checkered cloth napkin, worn and tattered from overuse. Feeling like the napkin, she tramped up the stairs to her usual room on the third floor. Hardly her first tryst, Fiona didn't care if the overnight guest still slept. Her key in the noisy lock, a door that screeched, the same door slammed shut, and the noise of a muffin plate as it slammed the top of an old wooden dresser didn't matter.

Her entrance forced his bloodshot eyes to open. They fluttered like the wings of a desperate bat, neither creature wanting to see the light of day. She watched, unseen, from her location near the sun-bathed window and studied his painful, morning-after, movements. Fiona rolled her eyes and grimaced as John Wells panicked, grabbed for his pants, and verified that his money had not been stolen. Last night, he flaunted the fistful of half dollars as if baiting a catfish. Fiona nibbled and then bit hard but regretted her decision by morning.

John's head drooped as he pulled at his hair with both hands and grumbled, "Where's the pot?"

She pointed between his legs to a spot underneath the bed and then turned back to the window, with her view of the street below. She followed a young couple walking, the woman's hand tucked safely in the crook of her man's arm. Perhaps they were recently married, she thought. They exited the general store, and he carried several packages, the smile on her face as bright as the beautiful, green dress she wore. The man smiled back. Without warning, the happy couple crossed the street and vanished from Fiona's field of vision. In an instant, they disappeared, like Fiona's dreams of long ago when she looked young and beautiful and innocent. Older now, much older, Fiona no longer claimed beauty or innocence. Instead, she wore bitterness like an unwashed, black and baggy dress.

"I paid for the room, you owe me that much at least," she said.

A sly smile crossed John's face. He reached for his shirt.

"I don't remember promising you anything last night," he said.

"You passed out you fool. Nothing happened."

John grabbed two coins from his pocket and tossed them on the floor like scraps of food for a dog. She scooped up the money and slammed the door on her way out.

John, fully dressed, sat on the edge of his bed at the Ausable House.

Unwilling to brave the wind and snow, he preferred to pout about his last day of work at the Split Rock Mine. He mentally replayed old man Scroggin's final words for the umpteenth time.

"You're nothing but a drunkard, John Wells, now please leave."

The voice reverberated in John's head like an echo in a canyon. He argued with the ghost as if it made a difference.

"Ten hours in a dark hole. What am I supposed to drink? Tea?"

After a few minutes of mumbling, John declared victory in the discussion with himself, retrieved his coat, and walked out of the room. He wore the same soiled clothes he wore yesterday but with an extra layer of defiance. As he walked down the narrow hallway toward the stairwell, he noticed the wallpaper, both walls covered with scores of perfectly formed pink roses on a lush field of green. It reminded him of his perfect, little brother. Delicate. Fine in appearance. Popular. And loved by all. John snarled and yelled at his dainty audience.

"And you, my dear Isaac, ain't going to no damn law school."

Cursing, he stumbled out the Ausable House door.

His long walk to the farm, just beginning, John spied a horse and rider. They headed in his direction at full gallop. When the rider got closer, John recognized the young man as Isaac's good friend, Matt Burns. Burns lived on the road to Port Kent at the same four corners occupied by Wells' farm, but across the road and east. John used both arms to wave the duo to a stop. The horse dragged its rear hooves through the snow and ice to placate its rider who pulled on the reins with all of his weight. John, stepped to one side, too hungover to care about his near collision with a fifteen-hundred-pound animal.

"Where you goin' in such an all-fired hurry?" he asked.

Burns, just one year younger than Wells, dutifully explained while struggling to catch his breath:

"It's your father. He's sick and in a bad way."

John stopped Burns because he wanted a ride home. However, the unexpected news about his old man offered much more promise than riding double on a horse. Now, John's brain ran at a full gallop. In his unconscious mind, the alcoholic son pronounced his father dead. Life without the old man meant complete control of the farm and his father's cashbox. Abraham kept it in his bedroom. The old farmer saved at least a thousand dollars, maybe more. If he died,

John would take it. But the older brother's fast-moving train of evil thought ran off the tracks when Burns interrupted.

"Isaac sent me to fetch Doc McLean," said Matt.

"Yes, of course," John stammered, trying hard to look concerned.

He forced himself to focus and recalled that the doctor would most likely want to use his own horse and buggy. John still wanted a ride home.

"You go with the doc; I'll ride ahead and let Isaac know you're on the way."

Burns didn't think to tell his neighbor what happened to the old farmer but then John didn't care enough to ask. His only concern was the outcome. While trotting the old mare, John contemplated the range of possibilities that would occur when his father died. Almost all of the scenarios had a happy ending.

For John at least.

When his older brother walked into the parlor, Isaac looked up, wide-eyed and mouth opened.

John lived at a boarding house near the mine, for most of the year. Isaac rarely visited much less spoke to his brother, during all of that time. Isaac learned of John's unexpected unemployment from friends at the general store.

"John–I didn't expect to see you."

"How is he?" John asked, his tone almost businesslike.

The younger son covered his father with blankets and made a steaming cup of tea, but it sat on the light stand, untouched. The wood stove in the kitchen exhaled loudly, with a fire that made the ice-covered windows weep streams of cold water.

"He's doing better. Actually opened his eyes once," said Isaac.

John frowned.

"The doctor is on the way. I ran into Burns. Took his horse. He's coming with the doc."

"Are you home to stay?" Isaac was careful not to disclose all that he knew.

"Well *he* ain't gonna be milking the cows, is he?"

Isaac forgot how cold and calculating his older brother could be. With his father seriously ill, if not dying, Isaac began some calculations of his own. The boy's plan for law school could be in jeopardy. His father offered to loan him the money; John may not be so generous. He might even sell the family farm.

Isaac thought a bit more about his predicament and felt a faint twinge of guilt. He shouldn't be thinking about himself while his father lay unconscious on the sofa. And yet, the boy remained angry. Always dead last in the line of life, he no longer wanted to postpone his plans because of other people–especially his prodigal brother. It seemed like Isaac Wells might never have the opportunity to leave the farm and do what he wanted to do. Isaac stared with contempt at his brother's back, as the older sibling searched high and low for the bottle of whiskey which their father always hid. Although awash in anger and guilt, the noise of his brother's frenzied search for alcohol tipped the scales in Isaac's muddled mind. Truth be told, he pitied his sibling. John, not Isaac, remained chained to the family farm, and the older brother foolishly thought his freedom could be found at the bottom of a whiskey jug.

"I gave him a shot of whiskey," said Isaac, as he retrieved the bottle from beneath his father's blankets and held it in the air. John moved toward the spirits but then stopped.

"No, I don't need it. Save it for Father."

Isaac did not believe his brother's lie but returned the bottle to its hiding place. As he did so, the soft touch of a cold and clammy hand startled him.

"Father?" said Isaac, a surprised smile now covering the boy's face.

John looked up and glowered in the direction of his old man. The farmer's eyes now open, Abraham Wells lay there, dazed and still alive. When he recognized his boys, the old man produced a weak smile.

Isaac knelt at his father's side, holding the man's hand.

Chapter 2

A Tired Heart

"I will be with your mother soon, the good Lord willing."

Abraham's morbid reference to his deceased wife surprised both boys. The threesome enjoyed a rare dinner of hot soup and cornbread muffins, compliments of the Widow Burns, Matt's mother. The longtime neighbor, concerned about the sickly farmer, used her skills in the kitchen to show it. Isaac reacted to his father's dark pronouncement.

"Please don't speak that way, Father. You've been getting stronger every day."

The aged man, stricken just two weeks earlier, showed great improvement. He watched as his older son used Isaac's plea as an opportunity to remove the last bit of soup from Mrs. Burns' cast iron kettle. John also scarfed down another muffin–his third. Abraham ignored the older boy's gluttony.

"I want the two of you to accompany me tomorrow. We need supplies, and I would like to see my friends at the general store," said Abraham.

Isaac stopped eating and placed his spoon on the table. He reached for his father's good arm, the other one now useless, a direct result of what the doctor called a "tired heart." The younger sibling pleaded.

"Father, even with the buckboard, it would be a difficult journey. We can get the supplies ourselves. Please let us do that for you?"

Abraham looked to his other son. The farmer did not have to wait long for a response. John burped and then he barked.

"The doc said bedrest. You're not going anywhere. I won't allow it."

John's raised voice betrayed no emotion, only irritation. The family patriarch fixed his gaze on the dwindling fire in the woodstove. But it took John's harsh edict to rekindle the dying embers in the old farmer's soul. Abraham Wells erupted in a rage. The old man slammed his clenched fist on the table. John's empty bowl jumped into the air, and Isaac's spoon flew to the floor. The farmer's useless arm swayed like an out-of-control pendulum. When Abraham spoke, his voice boomed with anger.

"I'm not dead yet, and you will do as I say."

Isaac was motionless. John studied the stained tablecloth and chose not to look his father in the eye. Abraham whispered his specific instructions.

"We will leave tomorrow morning as soon as the chores are done. John, you will hitch the wagon, and I want plenty of hay and blankets in the back."

With nothing left to say, the old farmer decided to stand. But a weakened heart, with gravity as an ally, made it almost impossible. Isaac noticed and came to his father's rescue, just before the farmer fell back into the chair. Abraham was grateful to his younger son, for sparing him that particular humiliation, and cast a loving look in Isaac's direction.

He ignored his older son and shuffled off to the bedroom.

Abraham Wells traveled through time, during his visit to Keeseville.

The town he called home for all of his sixty-one years changed in so many ways. A half dozen manufacturing companies, two grist mills, at least a dozen retail shops, and five churches, now thrived in the small village. Most of that progress had yet to occur when

Abraham walked the streets as a child. Boardwalks to shield pedestrians from the mud and a beautiful, stone, arch bridge which crossed the Ausable River made everyone's lives easier. Abraham saw the irony. As his world grew smaller, his hometown grew in leaps and bounds. Although his mind ached with thoughts of the past, Abraham said little on the journey, safely ensconced in a front corner of the wagon, sitting atop a cushioning pile of hay but underneath layers of warm, woolen blankets. Isaac pulled the two mares to a stop in front of the general store in Keeseville.

"Take the wagon out back; you can load the supplies from there," said the old man.

His sons, one on each side, steadied their father as he climbed off the wagon.

"Wait," he said.

Abraham reached into his pocket and produced two small leather pouches.

"I'll settle up with the store; this is for you."

Each pouch contained thirty dollars, considerably more than the six bucks they earned each week as farmhands. They both stared at the old farmer, neither boy moved a muscle.

"This will be my last Christmas," said Abraham.

The holiday, just ten days off, weighed heavily on the old man. Isaac looked away, unable to thank his father. John counted his booty. The farmer took no notice of their reactions, instead, nodding toward the store and with some assistance from Isaac, climbed the small set of stairs. Abraham then dismissed his younger son, clearly intending to enter unaided. John waited until his father was out of sight and then abandoned his post.

"You load the wagon. I've got things to do."

Isaac did as he was told.

As soon as the wagon was loaded, Isaac joined the men. They were still standing, most gathered around the old farmer, greeting him and remarking on his amazing recovery. Isaac focused on his father and saw him as if for the first time. He wore a red plaid shirt, clean coveralls, black suspenders and an old, straw hat swung gently in his hands. Blue eyes, faded with age, wrinkled skin, tanned from years in the field, and thinning gray hair made the old man look older. Isaac continued to study the frail, old man in the center of the room. The father he knew disappeared.

Abraham, the oldest in the aging clique, enjoyed their fellowship, a mix of local gossip, area news, and politics–lots of politics. After the amenities plus a hot cup of coffee, compliments of the store's owner, the farmer settled into a well-worn rocking chair. His friends did the same.

"It's been too long, gentlemen," said Abraham.

They took turns bringing their farmer friend up-to-date on all of the recent news. They related some of the local gossip, they passed on the news about area farmers, and they became especially animated about the political happenings in Washington. Isaac devoured every detail of the news, but his father frowned when he heard talk that South Carolina might soon secede from the Union.

"They've scheduled a convention," reported one of his friends.

"Lincoln hasn't even been sworn in," said Abraham.

"It don't seem to matter," came the response.

A lively discussion ensued about the election, slavery, the South, Lincoln, and the possibility of a civil war. One man had an old copy of the *Cincinnati Gazette*, sent to him by his sister in Ohio. The paper included several excerpts from Lincoln's speech when he was campaigning in that city. Although the newspaper was now almost three months old, everyone clamored to hear what the successful candidate had to say. The man with the Gazette read aloud. Isaac sat on the floor near his father and as close to the warmth of the wood stove as possible. But the impassioned words of Abe Lincoln on the possibility of war, with the South, generated the most heat. They stirred a deep passion in the heart and soul of Isaac Wells. Lincoln detested slavery and opposed its expansion. If war became necessary to ensure the success of this man's noble cause, then so be it. Lincoln's words filled the air.

"Will you make war upon us and kill us all?

Man, for man, you are not better than we are and there are not so many of you as there are of us."

Isaac was stirred into righteous anger and could feel the goosebumps on his skin. Lincoln spoke to his heart. The boy-man couldn't help himself. He blurted his emotional reaction.

"I'll fight 'em! I'll go to war for Mr. Lincoln."

Some of the old men squirmed in their chairs, rockers stopped creaking, and the wood in the buck stove, glowing red hot, made no noise. The awkward outburst snuffed out their chatter, and everyone waited for the boy's father to speak first.

"Son, before you go to war, I'd like to go home."

The tired farmer's response triggered smiles, knowing looks, and then laughter. The outnumbered lad was forced to smile and eventually, he too, laughed, secretly wondering how the prospect of war could be so funny. As the group broke up, Abraham lingered over the goodbyes. Although no one dared mention it, Isaac sensed the finality of the moment.

Abraham Wells would not return.

When Abraham and Isaac were ready to go home, John Wells was nowhere to be found.

After making his father comfortable in the back of the horse-drawn wagon, Isaac searched for his brother. The boy took the precaution of looking backward over his shoulder. He did not want the old farmer to notice his first destination, Sample's Tavern. John Wells sat near the bar at a large circular table, his only companion a half-empty glass of whiskey. He stared, bleary-eyed, as his younger brother approached.

"You gonna have a drink with me, Boy?"

"Father is ready to go home."

Isaac tried hard not to irritate his inebriated sibling, but John snarled anyway.

"I'm stayin'," said John.

Isaac hesitated, unsure as to what he should do or say next.

"It's not like the old man's gonna miss me," said John.

Isaac thought he heard a touch of self-pity creeping into his brother's slurring voice.

"Get out of here before I kick your ass!" he yelled.

Isaac scrambled for the door, wondering what he would say to his father. He didn't have to worry. The cold weather and the warm blankets worked like a strong sedative; the old man had fallen asleep. Isaac climbed onto the wagon and grabbed hold of the reins.

He urged the two, old mares forward, the sound of their hooves muffled by falling snow.

"Hey, Mister! You don't belong here."

The angry owner of the livery stable in Keeseville yelled at John Wells. After a night of heavy drinking, the interloper selected a barn for his overnight accommodations, his only company for the evening, a jackass in a nearby stall. The owner prodded his unwanted guest with a pitchfork.

"Get out of here, now," he shouted.

John, although a strapping young man himself, stood smaller than his muscular landlord. The hungover trespasser wisely decided that a hasty exit is better than a sound beating. As he slogged through the snow and ice, John pulled up the collar on his coat to protect himself from the bitter cold. His frozen fingers found a few coins in the pocket of his trousers, enough to purchase a badly needed cup of coffee. When John stopped to remove the loose pieces of straw and hay which covered him from head to toe, he heard approaching footsteps. Before he could turn around, a voice from the past rattled his aching head.

"Mr. Wells."

John recognized the imperious greeting from his short tenure at the local schoolhouse, years ago. Edgar H. Putnam, the headmaster at the district school in Keeseville, looked the same. John, now a grown man, could still be intimidated by the short and stocky, gray-haired teacher. He turned to face his former nemesis, greeted by two black and beady eyes peering over a set of wire-rimmed spectacles.

"You look like you slept in a barn and you smell like a distillery," said Putnam, known for his eloquence but not for his diplomatic skills.

"Mr. Putnam," said John, now pulling hay and debris from his coat at a furious pace.

The former pupil spoke in hushed tones less his aching head split wide open, or worse, Putnam started yelling. In years past, the belligerent headmaster yelled at John almost daily and for many reasons. John quit school because of Mr. Putnam, but the schoolmaster didn't care, preferring Isaac Wells as his star pupil. John Wells didn't matter.

"I intended to call on your father, but I was otherwise detained. Is he progressing? Has his health improved?"

"He's better," said John, as he focused on his dirty shoes, unwilling to look the former teacher in the eye.

"I am pleased to hear that his condition has improved. You, on the other hand, have made no progress whatsoever."

John stood there in stony silence, thinking about the hot cup of coffee that awaited him at the nearby eatery. Mr. Putnam produced an envelope and held it just inches from John's face, blocking almost entirely the former student's view of the headmaster.

"Please give this to your brother, it's a letter from my nephew. He is attending law school in Albany and, at my urging, invited Isaac to visit the school and meet the professors. I am confident that Isaac will impress them. His admission to law school is a near certainty," said the teacher, a triumphant note in his voice. He slapped the letter into John's hand and fixed his gaze on the street ahead.

"Good day, Mr. Wells," said Putnam, steering well clear of the disheveled young man.

"Thank you," said John, speaking rather clumsily to that empty spot on the walk which Putnam had just vacated.

The former student waited until his teacher walked well out of sight. The rebellious look that filled John's eyes reflected the anger and frustration that had festered for years. John recalled, as if it were yesterday, an especially, painful beating by Putnam, the young student already serving a previous sentence for errors in his math work. The boy's punishment included an extra early arrival at the one-room schoolhouse, to start the wood stove. Putnam expected the building to be toasty warm when he walked in, each morning at precisely seven thirty. On that morning, however, no firewood could be found. Putnam forgot to arrange for its delivery. John Wells was punished, nevertheless.

Wells, forced to drop his trousers and pull up his nightshirt, bent over the schoolmaster's desk while a horsewhip sliced into his buttocks. The teacher, sweating profusely and out of breath, did not stop whipping his victim until too exhausted to continue the punishment. Several of John's classmates cried, others shielded their eyes. His schoolmates saw blood on the floor, on the desk, and on Mr. Putnam, but heard not even a whimper from the boy. That day became John's last day at school; he never went back.

Now, years later, Putnam accosted his former student yet again. In doing so, the teacher picked the scab off an old wound. John Wells still bled from the soul, and Mr. Putnam remained oblivious and without remorse. However, on this morning, John could do something about it. This time, the student could fight back, Putnam's prisoner was free to do as he pleased.

John fixated on his brother's name, the black ink on Putnam's envelope evidencing near perfect penmanship. Once again, John recalled his younger brother, the sibling that everyone thought perfect. The sibling he detested. John fumed, the anger in his chest screaming to escape. In his mind, the teacher and the teacher's pet hid in the same envelope. John trembled with anger now, his eyes twitching like a man with a nervous tick. His heart pounded in his chest, and he struggled to take a deep breath. A muffled yell rose from his throat as he ripped the note into dozens of tiny little pieces, throwing them into the air like a rock through a schoolhouse window.

He caught his breath. An eerie stillness enveloped the young man. He felt satiated, like a wolf after devouring its prey. In a strange way, the former student avenged his tormentor and delivered a serious but secret blow to his little brother.

John watched, in peace, as the cold wind blew his brother's dreams across the street and into a gutter.

Christmas Eve arrived after two days of frigid rain, reducing the Wells' family farm to a sea of mud and manure.

The animals struggled, their hooves sinking into the muck, as they scoured the pasture for soggy grain and waterlogged hay. John, desperate for a drink, sulked as his father fidgeted with an oil lamp in the parlor, because it did a poor job of illuminating his bible. Little brother Isaac lay sprawled on the floor, immersed in a weeks-old edition of the local newspaper. John refused to read any paper, a thinly disguised effort to camouflage his illiteracy. Instead, the older son fumed, with a hunting knife in one hand and a sharpening stone in the other. He repeatedly scraped his blade over the smooth stone, until razor sharp. The noisy exercise clashed with the occasional snap of an otherwise warm and whispering fire. John took pleasure in the results of his efforts but reserved his deepest admiration for the cold, unyielding rock.

In time, Abraham surrendered to the oil lamp and lay the Bible on his lap.

"Isaac, there is a package under my bed wrapped in old newspapers and twine. Bring it to me please."

Isaac immediately obeyed, placing the medium sized parcel on his father's lap. John, observing this, put down his stone but held on to the knife.

"It's for you," said Abraham, returning the parcel to his youngest son.

Isaac, his eyebrows furrowed, frowned and then smiled. John took up where he left off, but this time, with a puzzled look in his eyes and a much quicker scraping motion. It required a few seconds for Isaac to reveal his father's gift, a leather haversack. A shoulder strap for easy carrying and a fold over flap secured by a buckle made the device perfect for carrying all sorts of supplies or in Isaac's case, plenty of books and papers.

"For law school," said Abraham, with a feeble smile.

Isaac leaned over and kissed his father on the cheek.

John pretended to find a small nick on the sharpened edge of his blade, his feigned inspection of the weapon then interrupted by Abraham.

"And this is for you." said the old farmer.

In his extended hand, lay the pocket watch and gold chain that Abraham had carried for as long as the two boys could remember. John, glued to the sofa, focused on the timepiece.

"I don't need a watch. I mean, I've never owned a watch."

Abraham continued to hold his gift aloft. John crossed the parlor, removed the family heirloom from his father's hand, and studied it closely as he returned to his seat. After a moment of silence, he glanced at his father, stared at the watch again, and then returned to his father's side, with his hand outstretched.

"Take it back. You said yourself; you're not dead yet."

John sounded ungrateful, but he couldn't accept the watch. The timepiece was worth money. The old man wouldn't just give it away, he thought. The father and the son, as usual, existed in two different worlds. Abraham ignored his older son and focused instead on the nearby tin-type of his wife. The photo, taken just before she got sick, remained as the only image of Emma, in the home. For years, it occupied a place of honor on the light stand nearest the old man's chair.

"Your mother gave it to me on our wedding day," he said. "It is my Christmas gift to you, John."

The old man rose, and the boys watched in silence as Abraham padded off to bed. Isaac said thank you as his father walked by.

John was examining the gold chain.

When Christmas morning dawned on the tiny village of Keeseville, the sun's rays had secreted themselves behind a cold and wet curtain of freezing rain.

Abraham Wells, as miserable as the weather and feeling fatigued after a sleepless night, excused himself from church services on Christmas morning. He implored his two sons to attend in his stead.

"It always made your mother so happy when you went to church services," he reminded them.

John rolled his eyes, but Isaac submitted almost instantly.

"Why don't we go, John? There's usually a good spread on Christmas day when services are over," Isaac said.

Abraham calculated that the reluctant sibling viewed the promise of fresh baked goods more favorably than he did the Third Commandment.

"I'll go," said John.

Abraham grinned.

Each boy mounted his own mare, and moved slowly through the mud, snow and rain.

It would be a long ride into town.

Services at the Methodist Church occurred as Isaac remembered them: too much singing, too much praying, and too much scripture reading. He breathed a sigh of relief when the Reverend Hagar invited churchgoers to the feast that women of the parish had prepared. Brother John maneuvered his way into the food line, first. He filled his plate to overflowing and parked himself at an empty table, John's way of avoiding those churchgoers who used the season as an excuse to be sociable, thought Isaac.

Isaac wandered through the church hall and eventually queued up for a drink of hot cider. A handful of people remained ahead of him when he noticed the young lady serving the beverage. She did not look familiar to Isaac, but then Isaac rarely attended church services.

"May I have some cider, please?"

"Yes, of course," she said.

Isaac noticed her uncertain smile and speculated that the girl could not overcome her nervous demeanor in the presence of a man.

"My name is Isaac Wells," he said, confident that his social skills were superior. Unfortunately, the boy clutched the cider in his right hand, and wisely decided against a left-handed handshake. He stared at her, unsure of what he should do next.

"My name is Rebecca. Nice to meet you, Mr. Wells."

Isaac glanced behind him hoping to extend the conversation but not wanting to hold up the line. He remained her only customer.

"Do you live here in Keeseville?" he asked.

"My mother owns a boarding house here in the village."

Isaac studied the girl. She wore her long, red hair in a bun, tied with a white ribbon. A smooth, white complexion, with a sprinkling of freckles and high cheek-bones, framed a delicate nose. She stood a little over five feet tall, with blue-green eyes, and a touch of sadness in her demeanor. When she returned his gaze, the boy looked away, pretending to verify nobody else waited for a drink. He did not want to be caught staring.

"I've not seen you in church before," Isaac said.

"My mother and I attend services every Sunday. I've not seen you in church before," she countered.

Isaac winced, his face turning just a few shades lighter than her hair. His social skills needed work. She leaned to one side, an older couple now standing behind Isaac and waiting for their drink.

"Excuse me," she said, forcing the boy to step out of line.

She focused on her task as several more churchgoers lined up for the sweet drink. Isaac shuffled off, turning back for a quick glance. When their eyes met, she looked down at her large bowl and poured a glass of cider for an unseen customer. Isaac grinned and contemplated how he might speak with her again.

"Have you accepted my nephew's invitation?"

He turned toward the voice and smiled.

"Happy Christmas, Mr. Putnam, but I'm afraid I don't know what you're talking about," said Isaac.

Putnam scowled, as only an old school teacher could, and launched into a lengthy explanation of his nephew's invitation. His diatribe included an unfavorable reference to the intended courier, Isaac's brother. Isaac grimaced at the mention of his older sibling but quickly recovered, elated with the invitation to visit Albany. He questioned how his school work could be accomplished while out of town. Mr. Putnam explained, but then stopped in mid-sentence. The aged teacher now glared at something on the far side of the room. Isaac turned to look.

They both watched as John Wells exited.

John did not want to explain the missing letter to Isaac.

Instead, he raced back to the farm, leaving his brother at the Christmas gathering. He walked into the farmhouse and found his father sitting at the kitchen table, papers in front of him, a pencil in his hand, and the cash box open. John pretended not to notice any of it, taking a chair beside his father.

"Father, we have to talk."

"Where's your brother?"

"He wanted to stay, and I wanted to talk to you–alone."

The old farmer nodded. John took a deep breath and started in.

"Last night you gave me your pocket watch. It's bothered me ever since. I don't deserve a Christmas gift, and I shouldn't be carrying that watch around. I know you're disappointed in me and I don't blame you. I haven't been much of a son."

John's eyes, downcast, focused on his own fidgeting hands. Then he looked up, just for an instant, to confirm that his penitential rite had the desired effect. Abraham's steady gaze revealed nothing. The boy continued.

"I'm returning the watch," said John, placing the watch and gold chain on the table.

"But I would like a chance to earn it back. I'm gonna stop drinking, I'm gonna do my share of the chores around here, and I'm gonna try to be a better son. And a better brother, too."

The contrite child finished with his spiel and waited quietly for

Abraham's reaction. The farmer's continued silence rattled John. The young man fidgeted some more. Abraham looked up.

"No, I won't take it back."

He grabbed John's hand and shoved the watch into the boy's palm.

"Son, I've been praying on you for a very long time. And I don't know if you meant all those things you just said, so I'm going to keep on praying. But I want you to say it. Say it to my face and swear it on your mother's grave. Are you being truthful? Have my prayers been answered?"

John refused to look his father in the eye, whispering his response instead.

"Yes, Father, your prayers have been answered."

When Abraham said nothing, John exhaled loudly.

His ruse had worked.

Christmas day came to an end and, except for a few stragglers, the church hall was now empty.

Rebecca Lobdell, no longer serving churchgoers, busied herself, scraping plates and cleaning tables. In the corner and by himself, sat the young man she met in the cider line. He would not take his eyes off her. His was the last table to be cleaned and she approached. "We meet again," said Isaac.

"Are you finished?" she motioned toward the empty glass and the dirty plate.

"No. Please, can you sit for just a moment?"

Rebecca looked behind her as if needing someone to approve. An older woman studied the teen couple from her vantage point across the room and then nodded. The girl stole one more glance at the matronly woman and then sat down.

"My name is Isaac," he repeated.

Rebecca smiled.

"Yes, I remember."

Isaac pointed toward the older woman.

"Is that your mother?"

Rebecca folded her arms and pursed her lips.

"Yes, I'm almost seventeen years old, but my mother treats me like I'm twelve."

"Where is your father?" he asked.

His inquiry surprised the girl. She thought for a moment.

"He was killed, well, he died when I was twelve. But he was my stepfather, not my real father."

"I lost my mother when I was twelve," said Isaac.

"How old are you?" she asked.

"I'll be eighteen in February. I hope to go to law school in the fall."

Rebecca, impressed but uncomfortable, did not finish her education. Her mother schooled the child at home, from the age of twelve.

"I've been invited to Albany to visit the law school. I'm taking a steamboat and then a train."

"First time on a steamer?" she asked.

Isaac looked at his empty cider glass.

"Yes."

"And the train?" she persisted. "First time on a train?"

Isaac's eyes floated to the ceiling.

"I suppose you ride on boats and trains all the time?"

"As a matter of fact, I've taken a steamer to Canada and a train to Canada, twice."

Rebecca smiled, enjoying their silly game of one-upmanship. She interpreted Isaac's silence as his admission of defeat and couldn't resist a trick question.

"Will you be attending church services next Christmas?"

In truth, Rebecca wanted to see the boy again.

"No, I mean, I hope to attend church services more often."

"That would be nice," she said, deliberately leaving him to guess whether she was referring to their next meeting or his attendance at church services.

"She has work to do young man."

Rebecca's mother stood over the young couple focusing her stern look on the boy.

Isaac stood and nodded his understanding.

"Yes, ma'am," he said, as Rebecca also rose to leave.

She turned back for a quick goodbye.

"It was nice to meet you, Mr. Wells."

"See you next Sunday," he said.

Chapter 3

Law School

John rose to greet his younger brother when Isaac walked into the farmhouse, the calculated gesture, designed to pacify their father.

"Isaac, I lost the letter that Mr. Putnam asked me to deliver. I'm sorry," said John.

The older brother attempted a remorseful demeanor, his only genuine regret, getting caught.

"Isaac, and you too, John, come sit with me in the parlor," said Abraham.

Abraham recounted his earlier conversation with John and announced to Isaac that his brother experienced a change of heart. Henceforth, there would be no drinking, John would happily assume his duties as the oldest sibling, and he would do his best to be a responsible and caring son and older brother.

"John has made this Christmas day a very special one for all of us," said Abraham.

Isaac arched his eyebrows.

"I am happy for you, John. This is a blessed day for each of us."

The youngest son told his father and his brother about the invitation to visit Albany and he spoke excitedly about his encounter with the red-haired girl, named Rebecca.

"John, I'm not angry with you for losing the invitation. If father approves, I would like to make the trip to Albany, and you will have to manage without me. Father, do I have your blessing? I have some money saved up. Please say yes."

"Yes, of course," said Abraham. "And I will provide the necessary funds."

John was irked that a portion of his inheritance would be wasted on law school but smiled, because his fake apology achieved the desired effect. Abraham interrupted the boy's thoughts.

"I am leaving the farm to the both of you in equal shares. As the oldest child, John will be responsible for the finances. I have set aside the funds necessary for Isaac's schooling. John, you are not to use that money for anything else. When Isaac is off to school, you will require some paid help. There is money to pay for that too. And you should still show a profit. Isaac, your share of the profits from the farm will be reduced by the cost of the extra help, unless you return to the farm and the extra help is no longer needed."

Abraham went onto explain that these provisions would be in effect both now and after he passed away.

"I have written all of this out and expect the two of you to abide by my wishes. Will you give me your word, as Christian gentlemen, that you will do as I have written?"

"Yes," said Isaac.

The older son did not respond immediately. His father's pronouncements were complicated and confusing. And yet, it took only a moment for John to simplify the matter. When the old man died, John could do as he pleased.

"Yes, Father, I will respect your wishes," he said.

Storm clouds gathered across the United States and on the Wells' family farm.

Abraham Lincoln, still waiting to take the presidential oath of office, witnessed a half-dozen states secede from the Union or begin the process. In the shadow of the Adirondacks, Abraham Wells, although cheered by his eldest son's apparent transformation from a treacherous spawn to the devoted heir, could not acknowledge the evil which lurked in the soul of John Wells. Despite promises to the contrary, John viewed his father and brother as nothing more than obstacles on the road to absolute control of the family farm and fortune. An addiction to alcohol fueled his ugly ambitions.

In the midst of these buffeting winds stood the devoted son. Isaac fell in love with law school and became infatuated with a young lady, after just one conversation. The young lad anxiously anticipated his inaugural visit to Albany but vowed to meet the young Rebecca again.

Like those Southern states which chose secession and briefly delayed a violent confrontation, so also did John Wells temporarily retreat behind a cloud of conciliation.

The tranquility enjoyed by Isaac's family and his country would soon disappear in the fog of war.

As he prepared for his departure, blissfully ignorant of the dangers which lay ahead, a child in a candy store could not have been more excited or more delighted then Isaac Wells.

A steamer from Plattsburgh to Whitehall and then a short ride on the Rensselaer and Saratoga Railroad would bring him to New York's capital city of Albany. His host would be Charles Cunningham, nephew to Isaac's teacher. The two already exchanged letters, confirming arrival and departure dates, plus a surprise. During the boy's visit, the capital city would also welcome the next president of the United States. In route to his inauguration in Washington DC., Abraham Lincoln would first address the New York State Legislature. Isaac, now euphoric, used a portion of his meager funds to purchase a new pair of shoes, a coat, and some clothes. His father's pre-Christmas generosity made the shopping trip to Keeseville possible. Isaac and his brother would take the wagon into Plattsburgh but first, the younger boy bid his father farewell.

"Father, you have made this trip possible. I thank you," said Isaac, kneeling near his father's rocker as the old man stared into the fireplace.

"I pray to God that you will travel safely and return unharmed," said the farmer.

"I'll be fine, I promise," Isaac said, with the confidence of a young man who had yet to confront his mortality. Abraham reached out with a trembling hand, grasped the boy's arm, and squeezed. And then he turned away, lost in the flames once more.

The steamer would leave its dock in Plattsburgh at eight in the morning. The boys left the day before, leaving plenty of time for the twenty-mile journey. After an evening at a nearby boarding house, John and Isaac found themselves on the dock, struggling with an awkward goodbye.

"Thank you, John, I'm obliged," said Isaac.

He reached out to shake his brother's hand.

John returned the gesture but blurted his objections.

"Seems like a waste of money to me."

Isaac faked a smile and changed the subject.

"Please watch over Father; I fear he will not be with us for very long."

The sibling ignored his brother's plea.

"I've got a long ride ahead of me. I best be going."

John walked to his horse and wagon, never looking back.

Chapter 4

The Journey

The steamboat, *Canada*, soon to celebrate its tenth birthday, appeared massive and luxurious in Isaac's eyes. Captain Anderson personally greeted his passengers as they boarded and shook the boy's hand.

"Welcome aboard, young man," said Anderson.

Isaac acknowledged the greeting, his gaze already fixed on the boat's accoutrements which, by farmboy standards, looked extravagant. The interior of the steamboat, no less impressive, included a chair in the sitting room which afforded the most panoramic of views. When the boat lurched away from its moorings and began the hours-long journey to Whitehall, Isaac watched with unblinking eyes as the backwoods of his birthplace disappeared from view.

From that moment forward, the boy did nothing but contemplate the scenic vistas and extraordinary adventures which lay ahead.

Isaac's maiden voyage on a steamboat could not have been more idyllic.

His journey to Albany forced the *Canada* into a contest with the waters of Lake Champlain, the lake flowing north, Isaac heading south. The steamboat required eight hours to reach Whitehall, an eighty-five-mile trip. From there, the young man took a train to

Albany. But first, Isaac's eyes feasted on the sensational sights that only a waterborne vessel could reveal.

Within minutes of leaving the dock in Plattsburgh, the boat approached Port Kent and Spit Rock, a promontory near the iron ore mine where Isaac's brother once labored. The landmark could not be mistaken; it towered eighty feet above the water's surface. As the lake narrowed, Isaac looked to the left and recognized the Green Mountains of Vermont. When he looked to his right, he saw the Adirondack Mountains, Camel's Hump and Mount Marcy claiming the lion's share of his moving landscape. When he reached Crown Point, the greatly narrowed waterway gave Isaac the impression he could extend his arms and touch both shores.

Before the ship docked at Whitehall, Isaac explored the steamer's interior. His accommodations were pleasant enough, but the country boy felt most comfortable in the boiler room, where hardened deckhands worked like floating farmhands. Besides, it was toasty warm down there.

The giant who shoveled coal worked as a freedman, manumitted by his North Carolina owner. He stood six and a half feet tall, weighed over three hundred fifty pounds, and greeted the boy with hands as large as dinner plates. He called himself Eli.

"My momma called me Elisha, but I learned Eli. Whole lot easier when I gots to write it," he said.

Without being asked, the Negro explained his decision to come north.

"They is no place in the big city for the black man unless iffin you work inside. I is an outdoh man and da boat is outdoh all day."

Between shovels full of coal, the black man educated his innocent passenger on the hellish life of a slave in the south, the somewhat easier life of a freed slave up north, and the only good way to fry up a batch of catfish. When it got too hot in the boiler room, Eli removed his tattered shirt, revealing a bed of raised scars that looked more like a mass of wriggling black snakes. The wounds, a horrible reminder of Eli's life on a southern plantation, shocked the angelic lad from Keeseville.

Isaac's eyes and ears stuck open for most of his trip to Whitehall. As he approached the village, he noticed a parade of boats, much smaller than his vessel, pouring out of the Champlain Canal and into the broad lake. Completed just four score years ago, the man-made waterway allowed a wide variety of craft to traverse it's forty-foot-wide lane all the way to the Hudson River and New York City. When the steamer approached its dock, the teenager, reluctant to leave, ran back to the boiler room. He wanted to say goodbye to Eli. In the midst of all that fire and water, the two became friends. Eli waved as the farm boy walked down the ramp and stepped onto the dock.

Isaac headed for the train station with a spring in his gait and a smile on his face.

Once on the train, Isaac nibbled at a slice of homemade bread and a chunk of cold chicken–low cost offerings at a general store in Whitehall.

From his seat near a soot-speckled window, Isaac kept a watchful eye as the wooded backcountry slipped beyond his view. In its stead, an army of residential and commercial structures invaded and then conquered the agrarian landscape. The train jerked to a noisy stop in Albany long before the boy wanted his steam-powered odyssey to end. As he stepped off the train, Isaac stood surrounded by a sea of sights and sounds that hypnotized the farm boy from Keeseville. From the multitude, there emerged a solitary figure pressing against his chest a square foot of brown, packaging paper, with the name, WELLS, scrawled in charcoal.

"I'm Isaac Wells," the boy said, extending his hand.

"Charles Cunningham and welcome to Albany. How was your trip?"

Isaac confessed to never having been on a steamer or a train. He struggled as his host gestured to an endless series of landmarks, during their walk through the streets of Albany.

"You'll be bunking with me. The room is free, but the old lady that owns the house wants a few bucks each week for the extra food. It's worth it, she's a good cook," said Cunningham.

Isaac learned that he would be visiting the law school early the next morning but responded with a happy yawn when his host announced that a good night's sleep would be their first order of business.

Isaac Wells bounced out of bed like his hair was on fire.

Today he would greet the next President of the United States. He would begin his adventure with an exploration of the law school in Albany. Charles leased a large room in a house at the far end of Green Street, leaving a brisk walk to the law school which the farm boy and his friend could easily handle. As the two men made their way down the street, Cunningham reviewed the inner workings of the law school where he studied for the past year. A handful of professors staffed the school but all worked as practicing lawyers. A student's regimen included formal instruction, daily classes, and a written test at the end of each term. Course offerings in real estate, wills, personal rights, contract law, and a variety of other subjects made the school year both interesting and challenging. And, for the first time, students received permission to observe court proceedings and legislative sessions.

"In fact, I have a surprise in store for you," said Cunningham.

"What could be better than seeing Mr. Lincoln in person?" asked Isaac.

"Attending his speech to the New York State Legislature."

Cunningham beamed; Isaac erupted with a war whoop. He grabbed his host and delivered a huge bear hug.

"I am so grateful, Charles, I am so grateful."

Isaac could barely speak.

"When?" he asked.

"After Mr. Lincoln arrives at the train station, we will leave early, and hightail it to the Capitol building. If anyone wants to know, you're a student at the law school," said Charles. Isaac nodded, more than willing to conspire with Cunningham for an audience with Mr. Lincoln. In Isaac's eyes, the new president embarked on a noble mission–freedom for the slaves. Lincoln deserved the support of the entire country.

On his tour of the campus, Isaac encountered one instructor and enjoyed mostly empty halls and classrooms throughout the visit. The boy, impressed with what he saw, noticed that everyone departed early for the rail station on Broadway. Isaac did not want to be left behind. The two friends headed back to Green Street.

"Do you have fifty cents?" Charles asked.

"Of course, what for?"

Isaac's host stopped in front of the Gayety Theatre. He stared at the playbill for that evening.

"Well, there's a reception tonight for Mr. Lincoln, about a half-block from here, at the Delevan House. I couldn't get us into the big shindig, so I thought we could watch a play instead. What do you think?"

"I've never seen a theater production, but the answer is yes. And you will be my guest. It's the least I can do in exchange for your hospitality," said Isaac.

The Apostate, a tragedy written in England, included five acts and several fight scenes.

"My friend saw it, loved it," reported Cunningham. He continued, "The guy who plays Pascara hasn't performed for almost a week. He was accidentally stabbed with his own knife. Tonight is his first evening back."

Isaac didn't know what to expect but looked forward to the evening of entertainment. He pointed to the name which headlined the playbill.

"Is he a good actor?" asked the boy.

Cunningham answered the question with a question.

"You've never heard of the actor, John Wilkes Booth?"

Chapter 5

The President Elect

Mr. Lincoln arrived on schedule.

His train, festooned with flags and banners, steamed into the station at two thirty in the afternoon. By that time, Isaac and his host pushed and weaseled their way to a spot near the speakers' platform. Isaac expressed his surprise when he saw only a handful of the local constabulary and no soldiery on or near the pre-presidential train. Dozens of men and boys took advantage of the omission to climb onto, over, and even under the rail cars. Lincoln, encouraged to remain on the train, until his military escort arrived, did as he was told. This gave rise to more jostling, confusion, disorder, and some outright fighting. The law student and his visitor enjoyed the excitement.

"I was here last October when the Prince of Wales came, and the crowds were even bigger," Cunningham reported.

"The soldiers are here," said Isaac, yelling to be heard.

The blue uniforms, forced to shove and push the unwanted guests, used the butt of their rifles, to clear the platform. A short, while later, Lincoln emerged from his car. His tall, lanky frame allowed the crowd to recognize their next president, but this man appeared hatless, sunburned, wearing long whiskers, and looking haggard. The young rail-splitter that most people knew was pictured in newspapers and broadsides, looking clean-shaven and with rosy cheeks. Lincoln, looking more like an imposter, received a modest cheer and triggered much confusion in the large crowd.

"That's him," Isaac screamed. "That's him."

The boy grinned as he hopped up and down, straining to spot that one face in a sea of hundreds. Cunningham reminded Isaac they had to leave early.

"We best be going if we want a seat in the capital."

On their way back to the Capitol building, Wells and Cunningham weaved in and out of the crowd which now lined the sidewalks of Albany. A horde of spectators formed around the entrance to the structure. The boys squeezed and elbowed their way to a large door. Two soldiers stood guard.

"Sorry, Gentlemen, you don't look like politicians to me," said the larger of the two uniformed guards.

"We're not. We are students at Albany Law School. We are permitted to observe the legislature while it is in session," said Cunningham.

"Not today."

Isaac, ready to comply, noted that the warrior in blue stood a foot taller than the farm boy. Charles stepped forward.

"I mean no disrespect, Soldier, but we have a right to."

Charles never finished his appeal. The soldier used his rifle, placed horizontally on Cunningham's chest, to shove the law student to the ground and down several of the Capitol steps. The guard growled.

"I said no. Now git."

Isaac helped Cunningham to his feet, and the two boys walked away, both brushing the dirt from the fallen student's clothing.

Feeling dejected and rejected, the two boys plowed their way out of the thickest portion of the crowd and slowly made their way down Broadway.

"Can I buy you a drink?" asked Cunningham, unaware that his teenage guest lived as a stranger to alcohol.

"Uhhh, sure." said the boy, who had been eighteen for all of eight days. The two ducked into the Stanwix. It served as a popular watering hole, less than a block from the Delavan hotel. The roommates sat at a table not too far from the bar.

"Whiskey," said Cunningham.

Isaac wondered if his apprehension looked obvious. Charles chose not to sip his whiskey, swallowing the contents of the shot glass in one swig. Isaac replicated his friend's behavior, prompting a fit of gulps, gasps, and wheezing. His roommate chuckled while Isaac struggled for air.

"You gotta learn how to drink, Boy, or you'll never make it through law school."

Isaac, feeling the need to demonstrate proficiency in his first assignment, asked for another glass and slugged it down, this time with only a wide-eyed stare to evidence the shock to his system. The boys grumbled about their defeat on the steps of the Capitol and used it as an excuse for several more drinks. When the alcohol forced both into a moment of silent stupor, a gentleman at the window grabbed their attention. He had been studying the crowds as they strode by, all of them supporters of the new president.

"Is this not a Democratic city?" said the stranger to his well-dressed companion. The companion replied.

"Democratic? Yes. But disunion, no."

The first man, handsome and sporting a well-trimmed mustache, shook his head and sulked. He rattled on, noisily at times, speaking ill of both Lincoln and the Union. All the while, he peered through the window at the large crowds which now cheered their new president as the tall man passed by. The diatribe irked and then infuriated the inebriated farm boy. Isaac, now emboldened by alcohol, decided to confront Lincoln's vociferous critic. Without warning, he leapt to his feet, giving Cunningham only a split second to pull the intoxicated teenager back to his chair. On seeing the near confrontation, the second man admonished his dapper friend.

"Mr. Booth, you must not say these things. In these parts, such statements could hurt attendance."

The boozy young men did not recognize the face of John Wilkes Booth, but they recalled his name. Cunningham grabbed his younger friend by the collar and dragged him out of the tavern. Isaac staggered to the door, reduced to shooting a dirty look in Booth's direction. A very mellow Cunningham waited until he walked out of earshot, to voice his reaction.

"It is my considered opinion that we shall not be attending the theatre this evening."

After another day of sightseeing, Isaac packed his meager belongings and prepared for the trip back to Keeseville.

The country boy, thrilled and yet intimidated with all that he saw, hesitated to leave. Law school in the fall seemed like an eternity away, and life on the farm offered no relief from the intense passion for adventure which now consumed the lad. Were it not for his ailing father and the charms of a young lady, Isaac might never have returned to his home in the Adirondacks.

On their last evening together in Albany, the landlady's chicken and biscuits induced the young men to venture no further than the parlor. Isaac talked non-stop about his destiny as a successful attorney, until Cunningham interrupted.

"You seem to have forgotten about the possibility of war," said Charles.

"I'm not afraid to fight those secessionist bastards," said Isaac.

Secretly, Isaac stifled that tiny voice in his head which questioned why he would ever want to leave home and Rebecca, for anything other than law school. Charles spoke as if he had already contemplated a disruption of his studies.

"My country comes before my education. If war comes, I intend to enlist."

Charles' somber voice infected the younger boy's thinking. Minutes passed as Isaac considered law school, his father, the farm, Rebecca, and even his older brother. The joy and excitement of his time in Albany had temporarily hidden the hazards of a civil war. The sound of cheering crowds and the smell of old books in a library could not erase the awful possibility that war would ruin everything. Isaac's world could disappear in an instant. The boy tried to cut through the tangled jungle of thoughts that choked his mind, but surrendered too confused and too tired to prevail.

"I'm going to bed."

Chapter 6

Mixed Emotions

The relative safety of his steamship did not prevent Isaac from drowning in a deep lake of confusing and conflicting thoughts.

In the short time they were together, Charles and Isaac had become good friends. As expected, the Dean agreed to Isaac's admission in the fall. Still, the innocent farm boy was uncertain about his unfolding life. His dying father, the prospect of war, a treacherous sibling, and yes, a young girl named Rebecca, were all pieces in the puzzle of Isaac's life. He wondered how the fragments of his future would come together and whether he would be pleased with the outcome. He wanted it all–law school, Rebecca, and the farm, but was that possible? Long before his mind had cleared, the steamer was docking, his troubled thoughts forced to wait.

Older brother, John, was caustic when he spoke, if at all, during the tedious wagon ride from Plattsburgh to Keeseville.

"How is father doing?" asked the boy.

"He's not dead yet, if that's what you mean."

"Did you hire some extra help for slaughtering the animals or hauling the trees we cut?"

"Well, you certainly weren't here to do it. It's coming out of your share of the profits."

Isaac's anticipated reunion with his beloved father was delayed until the buckboard was tucked away, and both of the mares were fed. The younger son was frightened when he first glimpsed his ailing father, asleep in the rocker. The old farmer looked emaciated, his face an ashen gray. The man's head was tilted to one side and forward, with no blankets to cushion, much less cover, his wiry frame. Abraham's breathing was labored, and he wore a pained expression on his face. The devoted son ministered to his father as best he could, receiving no more than a blank stare from the old farmer, for his efforts. After moving his father to the bedroom and making him comfortable, Isaac made his fury known.

"You have deliberately neglected our father. Are you hoping that he dies?"

"You were gone; I had work to do. What did you expect?" said John.

Isaac's anger was muted by his brother's accusation. Isaac had been absent for more than a week. He was partly to blame for his father's failing health. Still, he objected to his brother's change in attitude.

"But we agreed, John."

"I said what I said to keep the old man, happy. Leave me alone again and he won't be here when you get back."

Isaac shook his head in disgust as he entered the farmer's room and assumed his post on a bedside chair. The old man was sleeping, his face no longer twisted in pain. He looked small and frail and helpless. Isaac wrestled with the distinct possibility that his father might one day go to sleep and never wake up. It was a dreadful thought that made his stomach churn. The thought persisted however. His father might soon be gone.

And the boy wept.

Isaac put in a long day on Saturday because he would be absent from the farm on Sunday.

He planned to attend church services and hoped to meet Rebecca Lobdell, once again. Isaac rehearsed his greetings, his questions, his compliments and his stories, as he rode into the village. He wanted to impress the young lady. When the horse and rider arrived at the Methodist Church, he was thoroughly prepared. When he saw her, in the pew opposite his, she smiled. He ignored most of the lengthy church service, stealing glimpses of the young lady and then averting his gaze when she was peeking in his direction. It was a game of cat and mouse, but Isaac couldn't decide if he was the cat or the mouse. He caught up to her as they left the building.

"Good morning, Rebecca."

"Good morning, Mr. Wells."

"My mother is here with me, but I seem to have misplaced her." Rebecca scanned the crowd. Isaac neither required nor wanted a chaperone.

"May I walk you home?" he asked.

"You can walk us both," said Mrs. Lobdell.

Rebecca's mother had an uncanny habit of showing up when she was least expected. Isaac greeted her, but with a fake smile.

"Good morning, ma'am. Nice to see you again."

Mrs. Lobdell inserted herself between the happy couple and dominated the conversation for most of their walk. The modest boardinghouse where the two ladies lived and worked included a wraparound porch, with several inviting rocking chairs but it was too chilly to sit outside. Rebecca took the initiative.

"Mother, may we sit in the parlor for a spell? I'm sure you have things to do."

Mrs. Lobdell reacted with a look of disapproval. Isaac tried not to look guilty; it was Rebecca's idea.

"Yes, but not for long. Our guests are expecting their Sunday dinner."

Isaac, now alone with Rebecca, could not recall a single word of the script he had so meticulously rehearsed. The girl came to his rescue.

"How was your trip to Albany?"

The boy was visibly relieved and expounded at length on law school, the actor who despised Lincoln, and Lincoln himself. Isaac was ready to render his opinion about the prospect of war but decided that Rebecca was too delicate for such a serious topic.

"Is your father on the mend?" she asked.

She could see the sadness in Isaac's eyes, as the farm boy confessed his worst nightmare.

"I was not prepared to lose my mother, and I am not ready to lose my father," said Isaac.

Rebecca nodded.

"What about you? You lost your father and your stepfather," Isaac recalled.

Rebecca looked away.

"I never knew my real father; he died when I was two years old."

"What happened to your stepfather? You said he died in an accident."

Rebecca snapped her head in his direction and scowled.

"I would rather not discuss it if you please."

Isaac blinked and sat up straight in his chair.

"Did I say something wrong?"

"Not yet. And Rebecca has work to do," said the girl's mother, interrupting the couple once again. Isaac decided that Mrs. Lobdell was almost catlike in her ability to sneak up on the teenagers. The boy thought she would make a good hunting companion.

"Yes, ma'am. I was just leaving. Thank you for your hospitality. Good day, Rebecca. Good day, Mrs. Lobdell."

He considered a handshake but rejected the idea, bounding down the porch steps and waving to the girl and her mother as he left.

Isaac was pleasantly surprised when he noticed his father's empty rocking chair in the parlor.

The old man was no longer capable of walking unassisted. Isaac assumed that John had come to the aid of his father. Before he could remove his coat and hat, Isaac heard a loud thud from the direction of Abraham's room. Isaac poked his head through the doorway and surprised his older brother. John was on his knees at his father's bedside, a prayerful position, were it not for the open cash box on the floor nearby. Abraham continued to sleep, while the two boys argued with their eyes, neither of them uttering a word. Isaac retreated to the kitchen, John followed.

"Father is in charge of the money, is he not?" asked Isaac.

"All he does is sleep; this couldn't wait."

Isaac nodded, an artificial smile betraying his skepticism.

"It's Sunday night, John, what do we need that can't wait until the morning when Father is awake?"

"Go to hell."

Isaac watched as John threw on his coat and headed into the crisp, clear night. The angry brother wasn't looking to do chores, Isaac thought. More than likely a jug was hidden somewhere in the barn.

Another thump from the back room sent Isaac scurrying to his father's bedside. The old farmer grunted as he rolled on the floor, thrashing and tugging at bed linens that held him prisoner in a cocoon of cotton refusing to unravel. Isaac lifted Abraham to the bed but absorbed several of the old man's blows, as a result. Before Isaac could rearrange the covers, his father lay still and silent, his eyes wide open and staring at nothing. His breathing was shallow and weak. Isaac, worried about the impact of the fall, thought about loading his patient into the horse-drawn wagon, but it was much too late for a visit with Dr. McLean.

Instead, the devoted son donned a wool blanket and began his all-night vigil, in a nearby rocker. He would doze but could not sleep.

Isaac, exhausted from a sleepless night, could not rouse his father, much less get the old man into the wagon.

A quick search revealed that John was passed out in the barn and of no use to the young lad, now desperate to get his father to Doc McLean's place in the village. He galloped one of the old mares to Matt Burns' home just down the road, not bothering with a saddle. Together, the boys loaded Abraham into the buckboard, and the makeshift ambulance was underway.

Doc McLean suspected catalepsy and recommended a daily regimen of bleeding, whiskey, and small doses of opium. He listened to the farmer's heart once more and then motioned Isaac to the far side of the room.

"I can't be running to the farm every day. Can you find him a place in town?"

Isaac thought of the boarding house where Rebecca lived and worked.

"I have an idea."

Mrs. Lobdell, even less welcoming than she was on Sunday morning, refused to smile when Isaac appeared at her door.

"Mr. Wells, Rebecca is running errands for me, and I think it rather forward that you would come calling on a young lady in such an unexpected manner."

Isaac explained his predicament and noticed a sudden change in Mrs. Lobdell's demeanor. She preferred a paying customer rather than a potential suitor for Rebecca and became both pleasant and accommodating. With help from a few of her boarders, Mrs. Lobdell and Isaac relocated the old farmer to a downstairs room that offered easy access to caregivers and visitors.

"I can't be here every day and still get my chores done. I'd be willing to pay Rebecca to look in on him," said Isaac.

Mrs. Lobdell smiled at the boy, for the first time ever, he thought.

"Yes, of course. We'll take good care of him."

The days turned into a week and the weeks turned into a month. Despite John's objection about the cost of Abraham's daily care, Isaac's decision yielded results. Abraham ate regular meals, sat in his chair, and conversed with his visitors. Isaac and Rebecca took advantage of the old man's recuperation and enjoyed their thrice-weekly visits. The first week in April, being unusually warm, allowed the happy couple some alone time on the porch, Rebecca's mother away at a church meeting.

"Father is doing so well. Thank you," said Isaac.

Rebecca grinned.

"He's doing very well, and I must say he is a pleasure to be with. Always smiling and a different story every day. But he misses your mother."

"I do too."

"How did she die?

"Consumption."

"How did your stepfather die?

The blood drained from Rebecca's face; she looked away.

"Isaac, please. I can't talk about that."

"Why not?"

Rebecca sprang to her feet but did not leave the porch.

"You're going to have to trust me, Isaac."

"I do. Don't you trust me?"

Rebecca leaned in and kissed him on the lips.

"Yes, I trust you completely. Now go home."

Isaac, unable to move after her unexpected display of affection, grinned and stared into space.

"I said, go home."

Isaac smiled and did as he was told.

Chapter 7

War

John stumbled from the barn, anticipating a firestorm when he walked into the farmhouse.

He looked like he spent the night in the barn, his long, black hair sprinkled with bits of hay and straw. The bags under his bloodshot eyes framed a sharp nose made red by the constant consumption of alcohol. His pants, unchanged for days, smelled of cow manure and announced to passersby that he did not care about his appearance.

The empty farmhouse being a pleasant surprise, John foraged for something to eat. Finding nothing of interest, he decided to drink his breakfast at Sample's Tavern. Before leaving the house, he stole a few coins from his father's cash box and frowned when he noticed that both mares and the buckboard were gone. The kid must have taken their father into town, he thought, wondering why, but not concerned enough to give it more than a passing thought.

It was warm enough for the two-mile hike into Keeseville, and John enjoyed his leisurely stroll almost as much as he enjoyed his first glass of whiskey at the tavern.

"You know, John, you could own this place, with all the money you've spent here."

The admonition came from Jed Sample, owner of the tavern, but a bartender today because his helper never showed up.

"Go to hell, Jed," John replied, tired of lectures about his drinking.

"No. I'm serious. Have you ever thought of going into business for yourself?" asked Jed.

John tilted his head and looked away as if the answer to Jed's question was written on the far wall. The $1,000 in gold and silver in Abraham's cash box prompted John to think about Sample's suggestion.

"You thinking of selling out?"

"Well, I ain't getting any younger," Jed responded.

He wasn't getting any smaller, either, John thought. The owner, in his early fifties, was obese and bald. And he liked to flash two coin-filled pouches, strung together around his neck, wherever he went.

"What kind of money we talking?" John asked.

"Nine hundred fifty bucks buys everything–lock, stock, and barrel."

"Well, you make a pretty good living and you sure as hell don't work that hard," said John.

"If you get yourself a good helper, it's easy money. Besides, who do you know that doesn't want a drink now and then?"

"Well, let's see. There's my brother, my father, and my mother, until the day she died. How's that for starters?"

John was playing hard to get, but in his mind, the sales pitch from Jed was making sense. No more cows, no more plowing, no more chores. And all the whiskey you can drink.

"I'm going to think on it," said John. "Gimme another drink."

Isaac, stuck at the farm, was paying for his trip to Albany, John now absent for two days.

The younger brother accomplished most of the chores and rewarded himself with another trip to the village. The boy was focused more on his pending visit with Rebecca than on the horse he rode and realized that he loved the girl and wanted to marry her. The noisy crowd in front of Keeseville's only general store disrupted his daydreams. Isaac directed the old mare to the scrum and shouted his query.

"What's going on?"

"Fort Sumter's been attacked. We're at war," said one of the locals.

Isaac learned, that for now it was a war with no killing. Despite a day and a half of shelling, no federal soldiers died in the attack. The Federal troops surrendered because they ran out of food and ammunition. Ironically, it wasn't until after the soldiers abandoned their badly damaged bastion, that serious casualties would occur. Two federal soldiers were killed and several more injured, because of an accidental explosion of stored cartridges. After the attack, President Lincoln called for 75,000 volunteers and requested a special session of the United States Congress. A local newspaper was making the rounds, but the horde was getting its inspiration from each other.

"Are you going to enlist?"

The voice came from the noisy mob. Isaac scanned the crowd, until he spotted two waving arms. It was Matt Burns.

"They're organizing a company right here in Keeseville. I'm signing up. How about you?"

Isaac, still trying to absorb the news about Fort Sumter, responded with a confused look. Burns, awash in adrenalin, required no answer.

"Gonna kill me some rebels."

Isaac, not wishing to reveal his uncertainty, pushed any thoughts of Rebecca from his head and laughed in agreement.

"You'll have to get in line behind me," said Isaac.

Matt Burns let out a war hoop, hopped on his horse, and rode off at full gallop. Headed to the tavern, Isaac thought, where patriotism and bravery were sold by the jug. Isaac directed his old mare to Lobdell's boarding house. Mrs. Lobell and Rebecca beamed as Isaac approached the porch railing. Abraham, seated between them and tucked safely under a woolen blanket, smiled broadly when his son appeared, clearly enjoying his first foray outside the boarding house. Isaac barely greeted the trio, his news too exciting to be postponed. The animated farm boy enthusiastically recounted the news from Fort Sumter, casting several aspersions on Southerners, in the process. He predicted that dozens of young men from town would respond to Lincoln's call.

"I'm thinking I should enlist, too."

No one on the porch smiled, their muted response was like a cold, wet blanket on the fire in Isaac's belly. The wannabe soldier demanded an explanation.

"What? They stole our fort. We can't let'em get away with it. Don't you think we should fight back?"

Mrs. Lobdell did not return Isaac's questioning stare. She reached for Rebecca's hand and rose to her feet.

"Come with me, Rebecca, we have work to do."

Isaac slid off the horse and dumped himself into a rocker, next to his father. They sat in silence for a while, the boy too disgusted to speak, his father staring into the distance.

"My son, the soldier."

The old farmer spoke softly. Isaac sat up straight and strained to hear his father's words.

"You are prepared to die?" Abraham asked.

Isaac spoke firmly and with authority.

"Yes, Father, I am–for my country."

"And are you also prepared to kill?"

Isaac sat back in his rocker as if someone pushed him. The question left him dumbstruck. Dying for a noble cause is the definition of bravery, killing another man is different, unless it's self-defense, he thought. You know, kill or be killed. He wondered how his father, with just a few words, could stop the boy in his tracks and confuse him so easily. The old man certainly knew his son, perhaps better than Isaac knew himself. It took just a few minutes for Isaac to travel from certainty to ambivalence. Gallantry morphed into gloom somewhere between the general store and the boarding house. And the boy's bravery stumbled ahead on two cold feet. Abraham took a deep breath and exhaled.

"Go to war if you must, my son, but promise me that you will wait until I have joined your mother."

Isaac never ignored his father's requests. The mere thought of disrespecting the old man's wishes sent a shiver down the boy's spine. He could not say no to his father. And in a way, the farmer's request served as an unexpected lifeline for the boy. Complying with his father's dying wish would be the honorable thing to do. Isaac would have a plausible excuse for his warmongering friends. He wouldn't have to leave Rebecca and he could still attend law school. Going to war must wait, he concluded. Isaac breathed easier, his relief was obvious and his confusion abated. Isaac announced his decision.

"I will respect your wishes, Father."

Rebecca, listening quietly near an open window, deliberately cleared her throat. When Isaac turned in her direction, she rewarded him with a smile."

Isaac's last day of school, in early May, surprised him.

Mr. Putnam recited the usual felicitations, wishing his star pupil the best of luck at law school and predicting great things for the boy. Isaac sensed that Putnam's mind was elsewhere and took advantage of his new status as a graduate, to pose a rather bold inquiry.

"You seem distracted, my friend. May I ask why?"

Putnam's eyebrows shot up, and then he acquiesced to the boy's perceived impertinence.

"I suppose we can dispense with the formalities."

The teacher hesitated and then blurted his news.

"My nephew dropped out of law school. He enlisted."

Isaac recalled his discussions with Charles Cunningham during their time together in Albany.

"I'm not surprised, Mr. Putnam. He told me as much when we were together."

"What a waste. Any fool can fire a gun."

Isaac wrestled with his own mixed emotions. Law school, his father, and Rebecca were all good reasons to stay home. But his patriotic friends, willing to fight for their country, enlisted without hesitation. They seemed eager to destroy the rebels, unafraid to die. Isaac could feel a pang of guilt rising in his chest. He spoke in his own defense.

"My father asked me to stay. But I thought about enlisting."

"This silly war will be over before you know it. You belong in law school. Don't be foolish," said Putnam.

The schoolmaster's last words reverberated in Isaac's head, as he and the old mare pulled alongside two columns of volunteers, marching on the road to Port Kent. The recruits had yet to receive their uniforms, and only a few had rifles with which to practice. Isaac scanned the ranks, spotting several familiar faces. One head turned, snapped an illegal salute to his civilian friend and smiled. Isaac watched as Matt Burns faded into the long, dusty line of raw recruits.

Isaac's best friend was off to war.

Chapter 8

Demons

Rebecca fidgeted in the pew, inspected her dress, checked her hair again, and wet her lips, impatient for Isaac to arrive.

Plowing fields, picking rocks, and planting corn took priority over church services. She understood that, but three weeks is a long time to wait for your sweetheart. When Isaac slipped into one end of the Lobdell family pew, she burst into a smile. Rebecca then spent most of the next hour, peering in the boy's direction when she should have been praying. On several occasions, Mrs. Lobdell was forced to use her elbow to correct the unladylike behavior.

As the trio enjoyed their sunbathed stroll back to the boarding house, the young lady made a cheerful observation.

"Mr. Wells, it occurs to me that you and I have been courting for almost three months now."

Rebecca's mother made an unsmiling interruption.

"Courting is when the gentleman and the lady have agreed to be married. The two of you are simply seeing each other. You are not courting."

Rebecca frowned, recalling her first and only kiss with the young man. Mother was uninformed and incorrect, she concluded. But the sullen look on Rebecca's face remained until they reached the boarding house.

"Let's see how your father is doing," Rebecca said, the prospect of spending some time with the old farmer would be a pleasant distraction.

She reached Abraham's bedroom first, Isaac behind her, and Mrs. Lobdell back in the kitchen, preparing the old man's breakfast. The young girl stopped suddenly, using one hand to stifle a reflexive scream. The old man didn't move. An irregular bib of crimson red covered his nightshirt, the embroidered daisies which decorated the quilt now sprinkled with blood. A shroud of gray covered the exposed surfaces of his skin, the old man's eyes wide open and fixed on the ceiling. Rebecca remembered her last encounter with a dead person, her stepfather. He bled too, lots of blood. She turned away and pressed her face into Isaac's chest.

"And how is Mr. Wells doing on this glorious Sunday morning?" asked Mrs. Lobdell.

She squeezed past the young couple, a tray in her hands, neatly decorated with a cup of hot tea, a fresh cornbread muffin, and an embroidered, white napkin. All of it crashed to the hardwood floor when Mrs. Lobdell noticed the farmer's lifeless form. The loud and unexpected noise shocked Rebecca, sending a jolt of fear through her tiny frame. She pushed her way past Isaac and ran from the bedchamber. Her eyes brimming with tears, she stumbled to her room in the boarding house, hoping and praying that the demons remained behind. They didn't. A burst of noise, lots of blood and a dead man unleashed the beasts in her brain like a pack of vicious dogs escaping from their cage.

The sights and sounds and smells of that horrible night, years ago, lingered in her mind like the scent of Mrs. Lobdell's lilacs, harvested for the parlor every morning. The girl's stepfather drank for most of the afternoon and well into the evening. Mother worked in the barn, tending to a newborn calf, too weak to suckle at his mother's teats. The twelve-year-old girl lay in bed when the master of the house appeared in her doorway. Behind him, a bright fire in the kitchen's buck stove transformed his massive frame into an enormous, black beast. He shut the door behind him and stood over the child's bed. She could still smell the whiskey and the body odor, a combination of sweet and pungent that made her stomach turn, even today. At first, he took pains to be gentle, caressing her face and pulling the colorful quilt from her body, as if unwrapping a delicate glass sculpture. When he tugged at her nightdress, she resisted, and he became enraged. Despite his inebriated state, the predator demonstrated great skill. With his left hand, he pinned both of her tiny arms in place. With his right hand he muffled her screams, and with his legs and knees, he found his objective.

When finished, he abandoned the whimpering child and returned to the kitchen table, a glass of whiskey as his accessory after the fact. The girl lay there for a while, hurt, confused and afraid. A deep-seated fear enveloped the little girl, a gut-wrenching fear it might happen again. No! She couldn't let it happen again. She had to stop him. Now. She wiped her tears and rose from the scene of his crime. Anger swelled in the girl's heart and soul. She tiptoed to her parents' room, the girl's rapist still at the kitchen table, slipping in and out of a drunken coma. He looked up as she pointed the revolver at his head, not ten feet away. She thought the man had a surprised look on his face as if finding a gold coin on a dirt road in the middle of nowhere.

Her mother heard the gunshot. It sounded like an explosion, a stiff breeze magnifying the noise as it violated the cool night air. When Mrs. Lobdell flew into the kitchen, she saw Rebecca, still pointing the gun at what used to be her stepfather's face. But the blood that Mrs. Lobdell noticed most was the tiny rivulet that ran down her daughter's bruised thigh, partially hidden by the little girl's ripped nightdress.

Mrs. Lobdell took the gun, told her daughter to clean up, and approached the table where her husband lay, motionless. She disassembled the pistol, retrieved cleaning paraphernalia from the cupboard and placed a dirty, old rag in the man's hand. An unknowing observer would conclude that the poor bastard had been cleaning his gun. Then, she strictly enjoined her daughter never to speak of the incident to anyone at all. No one, ever.

In time, Rebecca opened her tear-stained eyes and recognized the faded, red flowers on her bedroom wall. Relieved, she used the washbasin to splash cool water on her face. As she pressed her flesh against the towel, she thanked God that the demons were gone. But they would return.

They always returned.

Chapter 9

Death

The fastest horse, in a small town, carries death as its rider.

Before Isaac could get back to the farmhouse, John showed up at the boarding house.

"I was at Samples Tavern. One of the customers told me," said John.

Isaac resisted the urge to roll his eyes in disgust. Surprise. Surprise. His brother was at the tavern. He bit his tongue and smothered the bad thoughts.

"The undertaker should be here soon. The preacher is with Rebecca and Mrs. Lobdell. They're in the parlor," said Isaac.

From his vantage point in the hallway, Isaac could see the old man over John's shoulder. Mrs. Lobdell and several of the female borders had already cleaned the body and tidied the bed. The old farmer appeared to sleep, Isaac thought. He turned back to his brother, their father's death a reason to be gentle and forgiving of past transgressions.

"John, did you want some time with father?" Isaac asked.

"He's dead, isn't he?"

The cold and callous nature of John's response was too much for the devoted son. Isaac shoved his brother to the floor, standing over him with clenched fists.

"If you weren't my brother, I would kill you with my bare hands."

John chuckled, rubbing the spot on his head that banged into the wall. Isaac, still hovering over his brother, restrained himself when the preacher scurried to the scene. The ladies crowded in, Mrs. Lobdell spoke first.

"Boys. Please. Show some respect."

I'll be with father," said Isaac, as he closed the bedroom door behind him.

John did not grieve; he returned to the tavern.

John attended his father's funeral service but skipped the reception. More than a hundred people gathered at the church hall, a sign of their respect for Abraham Wells. The platters of food, although tempting, did not slow John's hasty departure. He contemplated his first appointment. The newly-minted hired hand arrived at noon, Jed Sample, shortly thereafter. John and the tavern owner had reached an agreement–eight hundred and fifty dollars. Isaac would learn of the hired hand soon enough, but John wanted to keep his purchase of the bar a secret. At least for now.

"You drive a hard bargain, John Wells," said Jed.

"Count the money. I don't want you here when my brother gets home," said John.

Sample counted it. Twice. John waited for the results, deliberately shorting the tavern owner by twenty dollars.

"I'm short twenty bucks."

"That room over the bar, I want the bed and the dresser too."

"Fine, you get everything in the room. Are you happy?"

John flipped a gold coin to his visitor and then got up from his chair.

"Now get out of here, quick."

Jed Sample rode away with a smile on his face, but not toward Keeseville.

With the new guy, George was his name, more corn could be planted, more cows could be milked, and the job of cutting enough firewood for the winter would be easier with an extra set of hands. John could no longer be relied upon, his drinking now out of control. The expense of a new man could actually be recovered, and then some, thought Isaac.

Repeated knocking at the kitchen door interrupted Isaac's mental calculations. The boy's visitor, Widow Burns from next door, appeared agitated and overwrought. Waving a newspaper and unable to speak through her tears, Isaac forced the widow to be seated. She pointed to the paper, asking him to read it and sobbing all the while. Mrs. Burns sipped at the coffee he served, anxiously alternating her desperate gaze from his reading eyes to her coffee cup and then back again. The newspaper article was a lengthy description of the battle at Bull Run. By all accounts, the Union had suffered a bloody defeat.

"Matt isn't on the list of killed and wounded," said Isaac.

"But he was there," she wailed. "He's with the 16th Infantry Regiment."

"Mrs. Burns, the 16th wasn't at Bull Run. Look."

Isaac pointed to the paper, its print, small and easily misread.

"It was the New York 18th at Bull Run."

They both smiled in relief, Mrs. Burns requiring a second cup of coffee before her nerves settled. They chatted for a while longer and, in gratitude, she left the newspaper for Isaac to peruse.

The battle at Bull Run appeared to be the first serious battle of the war; four hundred and sixty Union troops were killed, another twenty-four hundred, wounded or missing. Isaac scanned the list one more time, taking special care when he got to the second letter of the alphabet. His eyes overshot their mark and riveted on the next paragraph of troops, killed in action. The boy's trembling hands placed the newspaper on the table, converting his coffee cup into a porcelain shroud.

Beneath it lay the name of his law school buddy, Charles Cunningham.

John arrived at his newly purchased tavern a little past noon.

Expecting to find the place all but empty, he came to an abrupt halt when he spied a single customer, sitting in a dark corner of the bar room. John blinked several times, refusing to believe his eyes.

"Good afternoon, Mishta Wells."

Edgar Putnam, obviously intoxicated and looking very much out of place, stared at John through glassy eyes. John sauntered over to the table and signaled his bartender for a drink.

"He's dead," Putnam said, struggling to keep his head upright.

"Who's dead?" asked John.

"My nephew, Charles Edgar Cunningham."

Putnam straightened his head and offered a sloppy salute to the nearby jug.

"I am his godfather, hence the Edgar. Or, I was."

Putnam had a fancy way of talking, thought John, but today, he sounded like every other drunk in town.

"What happened to him?" asked John.

"Bull Run. That's what happened to him. Bull Run."

John remembered the battle from conversations he overheard while in the tavern. He also remembered all the abuse he received at the hands of Edgar Putnam. Screw him, he thought. John's first instinct was to take pleasure in the schoolmaster's pain. But he didn't. John wondered why he even cared, but he felt sorry for the old guy. Putnam's head drooped forward; John couldn't think of anything to say.

"Sorry for your troubles. The drinks are on me."

Putnam looked up from the bottom of his half-empty glass and watched as his former student disappeared through a door on the other side of the bar. He drank the whiskey in one gulp, pulled a handkerchief from his pocket, and then cleaned his spectacles.

He continued to clean, stopping just long enough to dab the tears from his eyes.

The sun disappeared behind the Adirondack Mountains as Isaac stacked his last piece of firewood.

Preparations for a long, cold winter started at the beginning of August. Isaac looked with admiration at the long row of wood, stacked neatly against the farmhouse wall. One last item remained on his mental list of chores; he promised the Widow Burns some eggs. A family of foxes absconded with all of her chickens. Until she could afford to purchase more, the old lady needed help from her neighbor. The boy didn't object, she regularly delivered fresh bread and the occasional pie.

As he approached the Widow's home, a single light glowing in the kitchen, he heard a rustling sound coming from her barn. Isaac made no noise, placing the basket of eggs in the shadows and walking the grass that led to the side of the barn. He peeked around the corner, noticing the open door. That evening's sliver of moonlight left much of the cavernous structure in the dark, but Isaac didn't flinch. He moved to the doorway, waiting and watching for noise or motion.

"How are you, my friend?"

Isaac leapt backward, fell to the ground and searched the dark interior for the mysterious voice. From a dark corner, a man's figure came into the scarce moonlight.

"It's me, Matt, I didn't mean to scare you."

Isaac took a deep breath, smiled, and then hustled to his friend and neighbor, Matt Burns. After they embraced, Isaac took stock of his comrade-in-arms. Burns wore only a portion of his Union Army uniform, most of the buttons on the shirt, now missing. A rope secured the boy's pants around an emaciated frame. The soldier, covered in dirt and with bags under his eyes, smiled through his obvious exhaustion. Isaac peppered him with questions.

"When did you get home? Are you injured? When do you go back?"

Burns didn't respond. Instead, he walked past his friend to the doorway, searching the dark landscape and then shutting the door, all without making a noise. He motioned to Isaac, and they sat near a window, Isaac on an overturned milk bucket, Matt on the straw-covered floor.

"I was at Gaines Mills."

Isaac recognized the name from newspaper accounts. It happened months ago–not a big battle, but a brutal one.

"You got a furlough to come home?" asked Isaac.

"No."

Isaac squirmed, pretending the bucket made him feel uncomfortable.

"We marched through some woods to an open field. When the charge sounded, there was lots of hootin' and hollerin', but the rebs waited till we was halfway across the pasture. They just cut us down like we was hay in the field. The guys in front of me were dropping like flies. My friend, Jack, was next to me. A cannonball hit him in the face. Knocked his head clean off. The guy behind Jack was caught up in the bloody mess. I got sick. I was on my knees. My sergeant came up behind me and grabbed me by the collar. 'Keep going,' he says, 'You don't wanna be a coward, do you?' I got up, he gave me a push, I looked back, and he'd been shot–gut shot. He said 'Help me. Please help me.' Kept saying it, over and over again."

"His innards was on the ground in front of him. He was trying to put em back, like stuffin' in a turkey. I dragged him back to the woods, found a big tree, and sat behind it, the sarge in front of me. He was calling out for his mama. I must've fell asleep, cuz the next thing I knew, it was really quiet, and it was dark. The sarge was dead. I figure they thought I was dead too. I stayed in the woods that night. Next day, I looked for our camp. Honest, I did. I looked for the next three days, but all I found was the reb camp. I hightailed it outta there. Then it started to rain. And it kept raining. I was cold and wet and hungry. I wanted to go home. I traveled at night, hid during the day. Took me prit'neer three months but I did it."

"Does your mother know you're here?" asked Isaac.

"Yes. She says I gotta go back. They shoot deserters, but I don't wanna go back."

"I'm a deserter, Isaac. Guess I'm a coward too."

"I'd like a drink first."

Fiona rejected her new friend's proposition, a bit bold, she thought, for a drifter who rode into town less than an hour ago. He wanted to go upstairs, but she didn't even know his name, much less if he had any money.

"I'll buy you a drink. I'll even buy you dinner. And later on, perhaps dessert." He made the possibility of dessert sound like a question. He smiled, she didn't. They walked from the Ausable House to Sample's Tavern, picked a table in the corner, and ordered drinks. He pulled the chair out for her, and when the bartender came over, the drifter flashed a handful of coins, several of them gold. Fiona, feeling better about her decision to spend some time with the guy, pressed for details.

"You still haven't told me your name, Cowboy."

Fiona didn't really care, she just wanted to get closer to him–and his money. The drifter didn't respond.

"Good evening, Fiona, so nice to see you again."

She knew the voice without turning her head. It was John Wells.

"Aren't you going to introduce me to your friend?" John asked.

"You're drunk, John, you're always drunk. Now go away."

"Now is that any way to treat a former customer?"

Fiona wasn't blushing. Her face was red with anger.

"I said go away."

The drifter spoke in a low, smooth voice like an oversized cat, purring.

"You heard the lady; I think it best you move on."

"I own this place. Go to hell," John said.

The drifter stood up, reached for his drink, studied the liquid, and then returned the glass to the table.

"I don't care if you own half the town. I said move on."

John grabbed the table with both hands and flipped it in the drifter's direction. Fiona jumped up to avoid the contents of her glass but was too late. The drifter lunged and got a grip on John's shirt. He pushed the drunk owner to the floor, produced a hunting knife from under his coat, and planted a large boot on John's throat.

"I'm only going to tell you one more time, Mister. Move on."

The cowboy watched as John rose to his knees, signaling his surrender with outstretched hands. As he turned to leave, John stopped, pivoted, and then swung at the drifter with a closed fist. The stranger easily dodged the sucker punch and thrust the knife hand forward. John groaned and fell to the floor, a fast-growing bloodstain on the side of his shirt. Several customers rushed to separate the men; several more walked John out the door and over to Doc McLean's place. The drifter sat down and raised his glass to Fiona.

"He'll live."

Fiona, impressed with her date, flashed a quick smile.

"Care for some dessert?"

"What's so all-fired important about law school, anyway?" Rebecca asked.

She and Isaac were arguing on the front porch at Mrs. Lobdell's boarding house. Despite losing his law school buddy, Isaac still looked forward to his first semester.

"I don't want to be a farmer for the rest of my life," he said, growing increasingly angry with Rebecca.

"I'll be coming home for visits. It's not like we're courting or anything like that."

Isaac quoted Rebecca's mother, reminding the girl that their relationship was neither illicit nor inappropriate. As if to reinforce his thinking, Mrs. Lobdell made one of her unannounced interruptions.

"I can hear the two of you arguing all the way in the kitchen," she complained.

Much to Isaac's relief, Mrs. Lobdell sided with the boy, pointing out that Rebecca had no right to make such demands on Isaac, even if they were good friends. She added that when Isaac returned home, a successful lawyer, he and Rebecca could resume their relationship.

"God willing, you will still be good friends."

Isaac choked back his surprise. Maybe she liked him after all.

"I'm tired of being your good friend," said Rebecca, folding her arms, lowering her head and stomping her feet as she went into the house.

"I think its best you go home now," said the mother.

Isaac, feeling rejected and misunderstood, took the woman's advice.

"I'm sorry, Mrs. Lobdell."

As he brushed by, she stopped him with a touch of her hand on his shoulder and embraced the boy.

"Don't you worry none. It'll all work out. I promise."

Isaac left, troubled and confused.

Isaac rode through town and watched as two soldiers walked down the main street, stopping at almost every establishment.

The Bluecoats, stiff and unsmiling, crossed the road in front of him. They accosted several of the old-timers who occupied their usual chairs in front of the general store. Isaac overheard one old man pose a question to his seatmate.

"Doesn't the Widow Burns have a kid? Grown boy, I think."

Neither man was certain, but they told the soldiers that the Widow Burns lived on the road to Port Kent. Isaac trotted the old mare until he could no longer see the soldiers and then, spurred the horse into a fast gallop. When he arrived at the widow's door, out of breath and covered in dust, the boy gasped his request.

"Where is Matt, I've got to see Matt."

"I think he's in the barn. What's wrong?"

Isaac explained to the widow what he had seen and heard.

"They're looking for Matt," he concluded.

Mrs. Burns screamed when she saw her son's lifeless form hanging from a rafter. And she didn't stop screaming. Isaac, with tears burning in his own eyes, forced the mother's face into his heaving chest. Matt's body swung like a slow-moving pendulum, brought to life by a summer breeze and an unyielding length of rope. Isaac pushed, pulled, and prodded the hysterical woman, back to the farmhouse. They made it as far as the front porch steps, her screams now reduced to sobs, his tear-stained face covered with a look of despair and misery. The boy held the woman tight, repeatedly telling himself that the purpose of his desperate embrace was to comfort the grieving mother. But he, too, needed someone to hold him tight.

The sound of horses and a cloud of dust announced two riders. The blue uniforms, recognizable from a distance, approached the widow thinking that Isaac was her son. Isaac, with credibility that only truth can confer, corrected the men.

"The barn. He's in the barn."

Chapter 10

Pain

John Wells walked into the bar, exercising great caution and avoiding any sudden moves.

He spent the night on a bed at Doc McLean's office and was feeling the after-effects of sixteen stitches. The medical procedure included a small amount of whiskey as an anesthetic, but John's high tolerance for alcohol rendered the prescription useless. He sat, drinking at his usual table, nursing the wounds to his body and his ego, when the sheriff walked in.

Willard Bromley had been the sheriff for as long as most folks could remember. He was six feet tall, rarely smiled, and had a habit of tugging on a cold pipe when he was asking questions.

"Been looking for you, John," said the sheriff.

"Good, I want that bastard thrown in jail."

"From what I hear, you were drunk, and you started the fight. Besides, that's not why I'm here."

The sheriff explained that he went looking for John at the farm, not hearing about the fight, until he got back to town.

"Is there someplace we can talk that's private? This is kinda personal."

"Ain't nobody here, 'cept me and my bartender, what's on your mind?"

"Did you sign any papers when you bought the place from Jed Sample?"

"Nope, didn't have to. It was a cash deal."

"John, it wasn't Jed's to sell."

"What are you talking about?"

The sheriff explained that Sample had mortgaged the tavern and still owed the bank a little over five hundred dollars.

"As far as I can tell, Sample skipped town right after you gave him the money. The bank owns this place and everything in it. I'm here to evict you."

John jumped to his feet and then winced from the pain. He slammed both of his fists on the table.

"The hell you are."

"Calm down, John, or, I swear, you'll spend the night in jail."

"You're entitled to take your personal possessions. That's it. Nothing else. Understand? Here's the paperwork from the judge."

John ripped the document in half, gave Bromley a dirty look, and glared at his bartender.

"You're on your own."

"Sorry, John," said the sheriff.

But John didn't hear the lawman's condolences. He was already out the door.

Isaac, acting like a caged tiger, paced the floor, looked out the kitchen window, and then paced some more.

He didn't expect the sheriff's visit this morning, and he didn't expect that his share of the inheritance would be lost on the purchase of a rundown tavern. Isaac retrieved the locked cash box, now sitting on the table, but weighing considerably less than it used to. He looked again and noticed a horse and rider approaching the farmhouse. He could see from a distance, that his brother was in pain, but Isaac showed little sympathy.

"What happened to you?"

"I was stabbed."

"You probably deserved it."

"So, I'm told."

"How much did you pay for Sample's Tavern?"

"None of your damn business."

Isaac thrust an accusing finger and shouted, "I'm making it my business."

He reminded his older brother that each promised to abide by their father's last will.

"He wrote it all out and signed it. It's in the box. Open it. Now."

John reached into his pocket, pulled out a key, and removed the lock. He spun it around for Isaac to examine, looking away as he did so. When the younger brother opened the metal container, there was no paper and less than twenty dollars in coins. Isaac's knees buckled, and he fell into a nearby chair. John leaned forward, both hands on the table, his face just inches from Isaac's nose.

"You can kiss law school goodbye, little brother."

Isaac said nothing, sitting perfectly still, his eyes fixed on the cashbox. He looked strangely calm. Without warning, he rose and walked to his bedroom, deliberately, as if going to bed for the evening. But the noon sun was brilliant in a cloudless sky.

When Isaac returned, he had a loaded shotgun with him, pointing it at his brother. John wet his lips and cleared his throat. He glanced at the gun and then stepped forward.

"You don't have the guts to pull that trigger."

"Today I do."

The younger brother closed the gap between them and raised the weapon to eye level. He tightened his grip on the barrel and repositioned his index finger on the trigger. John stepped backward.

"Isaac, calm down before somebody gets hurt."

"What's the matter, big brother? You getting nervous? Have you figured it out yet? I've got nothing left to lose. Why shouldn't I kill you? You've taken away everything I've ever wanted. And now, you're going to pay the price. You're gonna die."

Isaac stepped forward again, John's back pressed against the wall. His arms were outstretched in front of him, the palms of his hands facing Isaac as if to push the assailant away but not daring to touch him. Isaac noticed the beads of sweat on John's forehead.

"Shooting you in the face would be too easy. How about I shoot you in the gut? Have you ever been gut shot before, John? They say it's painful and it takes a while before you die."

Isaac, breathing fast and on the verge of delirium, shoved the barrel into John's chest, pinning his brother against the wall. They stood there, motionless and silent, except for the sound of heavy breathing. Isaac's trigger finger straightened, he inhaled sharply, and the finger returned to its resting place. John's eyes were like saucers, his face now stained with tears.

"Please, Isaac, I'll make it up to you. Somehow, I'll make it right. Please, Isaac, I'm begging you."

Isaac's arms were getting tired. He lowered the barrel and his head slumped forward as if he were nodding off. He couldn't do it. He couldn't kill his brother.

He was Able, not Cain.

Isaac broke the shotgun, removed the shells, and placed his weapon on the kitchen table.

He threw the shells in his brother's direction, but John easily stepped to one side, avoiding the small projectiles, saying nothing, as his younger brother slammed the door behind him. Isaac started to walk, mourning the loss of his dreams and not caring about his destination. He walked for hours and finally collapsed in a mound of hay. The sound of buzzing horseflies and a barn owl, screeching in the distance, disturbed his fitful slumber. When he spied an inverted milk bucket, his eyes darted to the walls and the windows and finally, to the rafter. He was in Widow Burns' barn.

The soldiers did not dispose of the rope that Matt Burns used to hang himself. It remained, coiled neatly in the corner. Isaac walked the width of the building to get a closer look. He fondled the rope that put his friend out of misery, wondering if it would do the same for him. Death was so much easier, so much simpler, it had to be better than life.

"Oh, my God."

The Widow Burns rushed from the open door to Isaac's side. She yanked the rope out of his hands and flung it to the floor. Her hands cradled the boy's face as she pulled him nearer, pleading and weeping.

"No, Isaac, no. I won't let you. I've lost my son; I will not lose you too. I need you. Please, Isaac, please."

She wrapped her arms around the boy's waist, pressed her tears against his shirt, and refused to release him. Isaac, shedding tears of his own, choked his apology.

"I'm sorry. I'm sorry."

They stood there in each other's arms, unwilling and unable to let go. He spoke softly, exhausted from his brush with death.

"How did you know I was here?"

"I come here every evening, hoping to find my son," she explained. "He sent you in his place."

Rebecca sat with Isaac, in the parlor.

"The money is gone?"

She shook her head in disbelief. Mrs. Lobdell seemed to find all sorts of excuses to listen in, as Isaac related everything that happened. The girl reached for Isaac's hands when he described the aftermath of his confrontation with John.

"I was ready to do something really stupid. Mrs. Burns saved me."

The boy said no more, Rebecca didn't pry. Secretly pleased that law school was no longer an option, she chose not to dwell on the fact that Isaac's most precious dream died in a broken-down tavern.

"What are you going to do?" she asked.

"I'm going to work the farm as John's equal partner. And he's going to pay me back, whether he wants to or not."

Rebecca smiled her approval.

"Oh, and there's one more thing," said Isaac.

He rose to his feet and turned to face Mrs. Lobdell.

"Mrs. Lobdell, I would like permission to court your daughter."

Rebecca cried and laughed as Mrs. Lobdell hugged her future son-in-law.

Isaac left, enjoying the slow walk to his farmhouse. He frowned when he noticed that the barnyard chores were not done. He could feel the anger rising in his chest, as he walked to the farmhouse, convinced that his drunken brother would never mend his ways.

"John, you promised me."

Isaac stopped short, startled by the site of his brother sprawled on the Victorian sofa. John looked frightened as he stared at his younger brother through glassy eyes, his shivering out of control, and a sweat-soaked shirt clinging to his torso. Isaac could smell a putrid odor emanating from John's trembling body. He lifted the man's shirt and confirmed that his stab wound had become a swollen red mass, oozing pus and blood. John had the fever.

"Come on! We gotta get you to the doctor."

Isaac struggled with his ailing brother but got John on the buckboard and over to Doc McLean's place in Keeseville.

McLean shook his head, his dismay obvious, as he placed a well-worn, cigar-shaped piece of wood near John's mouth.

"Bite down on this, as hard as you can."

The doctor didn't give John a chance to think about what might happen next, as he plunged his surgical blade into the red mass and jumped back. His patient's anguished screams were muffled by the wooden pacifier, but a gush of blood, water, and pus poured onto the examining table and floor. McLean stepped into the blood puddle to clean the wound, yanking on old sutures as if they were porcupine quills in a dog's nose. John passed out from the pain, his limp and near-lifeless body acknowledging the doctor's ministrations, with nothing more than an occasional twitch. After McLean had cleaned and bandaged the gaping hole, he turned to Isaac.

"When he wakes up, he's going to be in lots of pain. This is opium. No more than a spoonful each day. I'm going to want to bleed him and check the stitches, can you get him a room at the boarding house?"

Isaac nodded and trudged to Rebecca's place, wondering why God had surrounded him with so much death. He considered the possibility that John too could die and, despite their differences, whispered a quick prayer.

"Mr. Wells, you may be courting my daughter, but it is not appropriate for you to visit anytime you please."

Once again, Isaac surprised the woman with his sudden need for a room, and while he secretly objected to using his father's death chamber, the boy saw no alternative for his ailing sibling.

After getting his brother settled, Isaac scurried home.

He had chores to do.

Chapter 11

Recovered

"Thank you."

Rebecca stepped back. She did not expect her patient to be awake. For three days, Rebecca ministered to John Wells, changing his bandages, dispensing his medicine, and assisting Dr. McLean during his visits. John regularly slipped in and out of consciousness, but on this day, he showed clear signs of improvement.

"You're welcome," she responded, uncertain as to how she should treat her boyfriend's nemesis.

"You must be Rebecca. My brother is real sweet on you."

Rebecca could not suppress a smile, but the girl was cautious and changed the subject.

"You seem to be feeling better this morning, Mr. Wells."

"John, call me John."

The girl did not respond; her mother was at the bedroom door.

"You have a visitor, Mr. Wells," Mrs. Lobdell announced.

The doorway was now blocked by a man with a sidearm. He tipped his hat in Rebeca's direction as she slipped out of the room. She paused at a hallway table within earshot of the conversation, pretending to tidy up as she listened.

"Sheriff, I didn't know you made sick calls."

"It's business, John."

Rebecca could hear the rocking chair creak under the weight of the sheriff.

"They caught up to Jed Sample. Found him in Albany."

"You're kidding. Does he still have my money?"

"They found him with a woman. She ran off with a chunk of it, but Jed had close to five hundred bucks in their hotel room."

"That bastard, I hope he rots in jail."

"I checked with the bank, they got no claim to the money, because they repossessed the tavern. As soon as I get it, I'll turn the money over to you," said the sheriff.

"I'll take what I can get," said John.

"Oh, and one more thing, Sheriff, this is just between us, right?"

"Yeah, I guess so."

Rebecca, warned by the rocking chair, scampered into a nearby room and fumed.

"That money belongs to Isaac."

Rebecca wagged her finger as she spoke, lecturing her mother, because Mrs. Lobdell seemed unwilling to weigh in on the matter.

"Child, listen to me. Do you think it wise to come between two brothers?"

The headstrong girl was not persuaded.

"I'm not going to hide this from Isaac. We are going to be married soon enough and there should be no secrets between a wife and her husband."

Mrs. Lobdell jerked her head up and leaned forward. She spoke in a low voice.

"Really? Are you going to tell him about your stepfather?"

"Mama, I was twelve years old."

"I know how old you were, I was there, remember?"

Rebecca recalled her mother's quick thinking on that horrible night. She reached across the table and grasped the woman's hand.

"Mother, I am not going to tell my husband that I killed a man–ever."

Both women stopped talking, distracted by a noise in the hallway. The floorboards were groaning under the weight of stockinged feet.

Rebecca avoided eye contact with her patient.

John Wells was ready to go home. She changed his bandage for the last time and helped John with his shirt.

"Thank you, Rebecca, you have been a good nurse."

"You're welcome, Mr. Wells."

The formality was deliberate as Rebecca did not trust her future brother-in-law.

"Oh, come now, Rebecca, you've seen me half-naked, can't you call me John?"

"Mr. Wells, I have never seen you -."

John used their physical proximity to his advantage, putting his arm around the girl's waist and pulling himself up off the bed. The movement forced her into it an unwanted embrace. He kissed her on the cheek, not caring that it was against her will. She shoved him with all of her strength, forcing the brute back onto the bed.

"Mr. Wells."

"Rebecca, it's just my way of saying thank you."

"Do the buttons yourself. I'm done here."

John, on his way out of the village, made a quick stop at the sheriff's office.

"Your money hasn't arrived yet, John. Come back next week."

"I know that, Sheriff. I just wanted to say thank you for your hard work. You got some of my money back, and I'm much obliged."

"From what I hear, Sample went to the sheriff in Albany County to file a complaint against his runaway girlfriend. Not too smart. I didn't have to do anything."

"Well thanks anyway," said John, as he turned to leave.

"How long you been the sheriff in town?"

"Going on fifteen years."

"Was you here when Mrs. Lobdell's husband was killed?" asked John.

The sheriff looked up from his paperwork and then leaned forward in his chair.

"That was an accident."

"Really?"

"Yes, sir. The man was cleaning his gun. Why are you asking? That's none of your business."

"No reason, just asking."

John returned to the farm, deep in thought.

John, unusually solicitous of his younger brother, busied himself in the kitchen.

The two men finished their chores and were taking a lunch break. The older brother offered to prepare lunch for his younger brother, something he had not done in recent memory. His motives were not entirely altruistic. While he was grateful to Isaac for sparing his life and then seeing to his care when he got the fever, John refused to abandon his ulterior motives. Staying on the boy's good side would avoid another episode with Isaac's shotgun, he thought.

The two sat at the kitchen table, nibbling on a piece of ham and chasing it down with some cool cider. September had slipped into October and apple cider was easy to find and inexpensive to purchase.

Isaac heard the sound of a horse's hooves.

"We have company," said Isaac.

John stood in front of the window and struggled to hide his panic.

Isaac did not recognize Sheriff Bromley, but John did.

"I'll see what he wants," said John, hoping to prevent his visitor from entering the farmhouse.

"I didn't get a chance to knock," said the sheriff, John deliberately blocking the lawman's path through the open door.

"You must be John's brother." said the sheriff, looking over John's shoulder while Isaac, now standing, was chewing on his ham.

"Come on in, set a spell," said Isaac.

John forced a smile, stepped aside, and introduced Bromley. The sheriff greeted Isaac with one hand and heaved a sack on the table, which was heavy enough to make the plates rattle.

"As promised, John."

"Thank you, Sheriff, I haven't even had the chance to give my brother the good news."

John saw the sheriff grin and wondered if the lawman's visit wasn't deliberately timed.

"Five hundred dollars is a lot of money," said Bromley.

Isaac focused on the burlap sack, his eyes growing large, and then turned in John's direction, a quizzical look on his face. John explained, talking faster than usual, and avoiding eye contact with his brother, until the very end of his monologue. The sheriff helped himself to some ham and grinned some more when John wiped the sweat from his brow and swallowed hard.

"Half of this is yours," little brother.

The sheriff interjected, "John, you never told me that Isaac was in on the tavern deal, fifty-fifty."

"I wasn't. This is my money. All of it. You can chase Jed Sample for your half, John."

John, ready to strangle the sheriff, watched as Bromley reached for a piece of ham.

"His girlfriend has the other half or most of it. Not sure we're ever gonna find her."

John was shooting bullets with his eyes as he glared at the sheriff and recalled his brief meeting with Bromley just two weeks ago. Clearly, the sheriff did not want John poking around into the details of Mr. Lobdell's untimely death. Bromley was sending a message, thought John.

The sheriff grabbed one more piece of meat, shoving it quickly into his mouth, so as to shake Isaac's outstretched hand.

"Much obliged, Sheriff," said Isaac.

The two shook hands. John slammed the door behind Bromley as Isaac poured the sack of coins onto the table and began counting.

Isaac gathered up his share and went to show Rebecca.

"Four hundred and seventy-five dollars?"

Rebecca and her betrothed were in their usual spot on the porch of the boarding house, even though fall had surrounded them with cool air. Rebecca cupped her cheeks with both hands and stared at the sack of coins on Isaac's lap.

"It would take me years to earn that much money," said Isaac.

"Can I hold it?" she asked, a giggle slipping from her mouth.

"You can keep it."

"What do you mean?"

"It's our money, Rebecca. We can have a nice wedding, maybe even buy a house of our own."

Isaac, dreaming out loud, placed both of his hands around Rebecca's shoulders.

"I love you, Rebecca Lobdell."

"I love you too, Isaac Wells."

"I'd like to get married in May," said Isaac.

She leaned forward and kissed him on the lips."

"Let's go tell Mother," she said, as each of them leapt to their feet.

In their wake, the rocking chairs were moving in perfect unison, much like the would-be lovers. But it was only temporary.

Chapter 12

Blackmail

As the Adirondack mountains shed their colorful blanket of reds and yellows, a cold wind swept into the Champlain Valley, warning its inhabitants that winter was threatening. John Wells had some threats of his own.

He knocked on the door to Mrs. Lobdell's boarding house, surprising the owner.

"Mr. Wells, I was not expecting you. Please state your business," said Mrs. Lobdell, eyebrows furrowed and a stern look on her face.

"I'm here to see you and your daughter."

The woman left John at the door and went in search of her daughter. They gathered in the parlor–John on a straight back chair and the ladies on the sofa.

"I want my money back," said John.

"Excuse me?" said Mrs. Lobdell.

"I want my money back."

John was focused on Rebecca, blinking repeatedly, and clenching his fists.

Rebecca's voice was shaking.

"Your father left that money to the both of you."

"Mr. Wells, I see no reason to continue this conversation," said Mrs. Lobdell, rising to her feet.

"How bout I give you a reason?"

The woman stopped and gave the man a chance to explain.

"I know what happened to your late husband."

Mrs. Lobdell collapsed onto the sofa, grabbing Rebecca's arm for balance. Rebecca hissed.

"It was you in the hallway."

John flashed a wicked smile, proud of his underhanded methods. But he wanted the girl to squirm.

"He wasn't cleaning his gun, was he Rebecca?"

John could see the tears filling her eyes.

"You don't have to tell your future husband that you killed a man but you may have to answer the sheriff's questions."

Mrs. Lobdell sobbed.

"You don't understand," she said.

"I do understand. You have my money, and I want it back. Now."

When neither of the women moved, John stood up for his final peroration. It was short but devastating.

"The way I see it, you're both going to jail."

"Wait," said the older woman.

"Rebecca, give him what he wants."

When she returned, the girl refused to surrender the money to her blackmailer giving it to Mrs. Lobdell instead.

John yanked it from the woman's hands and left.

The Christmas holiday came and went without incident.

John's thirst for money, at least temporarily satiated, plus his brother's ignorance of the storm to come, made for a peaceful coexistence. The blackmailer's victims were frozen in time, not unlike the small lakes and ponds which dotted the North Country, beautiful to behold but fraught with danger in the spring.

As the snows melted and the dirty brown color of a dying winter gave way to patches of green and bud-filled trees, Isaac's thoughts turned to his upcoming wedding. Rebecca, uncharacteristically restrained about the affair, said little or nothing about her dress, their guests, or even the exact date. Isaac thought that women of all ages became delirious with joy when the subject of a wedding first surfaced. He questioned Rebecca and discovered the reason for her reluctance.

"I don't want to move to Albany."

Rebecca and Isaac shared the sofa in Mrs. Lobdell's parlor, but they were miles apart. Isaac reminded her that his dream of law school was postponed, not canceled. With the money in hand, his continued studies were now possible.

"I don't understand. Why are you acting like this?" Isaac pleaded.

The boy was flustered and confused. It didn't seem to matter what he said. Rebecca's arms were folded, her teeth clenched.

"I'm not your slave. You can't order me around like a hired hand," she said.

"Rebecca, you're acting like a little girl. Why can't you listen to reason?"

"I am not a little girl and you, Mr. Wells, will not address me in that fashion, ever again."

I'll address you any way I want."

"No, you won't."

Rebecca stomped out of the room, with Isaac just a few steps behind.

Rebecca Lobdell, don't you walk away from me. I am your future husband."

"Not anymore. The wedding's off."

Isaac left.

Isaac, in search of a drink, peered through a crack in the boarded window at Sample's Tavern.

He walked some more, remembering that the Ausable House served beer in their dining room. The house Negro made his third trip to Isaac's table when a lady's voice interrupted his depression.

"You look like someone I know."

"Evening, ma'am."

"Mind if I join you?" she asked.

The woman was carrying her own drink. Isaac saw no reason to object and motioned to the chair.

"My name is Fiona."

She extended her hand, Isaac gave it a polite squeeze.

"Do you have a name?"

"Isaac."

"You're John's little brother."

Isaac's eyes rolled to the top of his head. He gulped hard and studied the red, checkered tablecloth.

"Lemme guess, you think he's a drunk and a scoundrel."

"I know some drunks, who would be insulted by that comparison."

Isaac chuckled, surprised that any woman, much less a barmaid, would be so eloquent.

"What's your name again?" Isaac asked.

"Fiona Dunham."

He studied her for a moment. Blond hair, blue eyes, pouty lips, costume jewelry that dangled from her ears and an attitude, as obvious as the bosom underneath her tight-fitting, red dress. He gave no thought to her friendly demeanor. She regaled the intoxicated boy with her stories of bar-room brawls, lovers' spats and violent wives. When it was his turn, Isaac confessed to shattered dreams, a treacherous brother, and a lost love. They talked for several hours, a cold wind now blowing in the darkness.

"Isaac, I have a room here, why not spend the night? Just a place to sleep. Nothing else. I promise."

Isaac, touched by her genuine concern, gave no thought to the circumstances of their meeting and accepted her invitation. He wanted someone to talk to, someone who understood. On that night, Fiona Dunham fulfilled all of his simple requirements.

Isaac passed out when his head hit the pillow, but he woke up in the middle of the night, with a woman in his bed. She stirred and reflexively put her arms around the young man. He inhaled the cheap perfume and returned her embrace. A few hours of sleep left him sober enough to be aroused, inebriated enough to shed his inhibitions. She assisted him when he discarded his clothes, guided him when his innocence required it and submitted when their lust demanded it.

When the sun had risen enough to bathe their bed in a warm glow, he opened his eyes to an empty room. Isaac could not recall how he arrived in that place but he remembered what happened in that place. Still innocent in his thinking, the young man was drowning in guilt as he dressed, wondering about the woman who called herself Fiona. He didn't mean to take advantage of her, it just happened. He watched, wide-eyed, as the door slowly opened, the person on the other side taking great pains to minimize the noise from its squeaky hinges. It was her.

"Fiona, it wasn't my intention to . . ."

She shook her head, rushed to his side and dropping to her knees, silenced the boy with a gentle touch of her hand on his lips.

"I know. And believe it or not, it wasn't my intention, either. It just happened."

She rose, kissed him on the forehead and placed a red-checkered napkin with muffins tucked inside, onto his lap.

"Something for the road."

"Thank you," he said.

"No. I thank you, Isaac. It's been a long time since I spent an evening with a gentleman."

Isaac thought she was about to cry. And then she left the room.

Isaac slow-walked his horse down the main street in Keeseville, not wanting to go home and unwilling to see Rebecca again.

He didn't see Mr. Putnam emerging from the dry goods store and was startled by the schoolmaster's greeting.

"Mr. Wells, are you, have you been drinking?"

"I'm sorry, Mr. Putnam, it's not what you think."

"You smell like your brother."

"Mr. Putnam, I can explain."

"I'm not going to support your admission to law school, if your intentions are to spend your time in the nearest bar."

"But, Mr. Putnam."

"You, in particular, have seen the destructive effects of alcohol in your own family, I thought you were smarter than that, Mr. Wells."

Isaac, upset with Rebecca, still angry with John, and feeling guilty about his unplanned rendezvous with Fiona, blocked his ears with both hands and screamed.

"No. No. You don't understand."

"I understand perfectly well, Mr. Wells, and the Dean of Albany Law School will also understand when he gets my letter."

Isaac clenched his fists, no longer willing to respond. Putnam, still babbling, poked the boy's chest, humiliating Isaac and triggering a flood of adrenalin. Isaac hit Putnam as hard as he could and watched, as Putnam went sprawling onto the boardwalk, his spectacles flying into the gutter. For a moment, the teacher and student didn't move.

Isaac, shocked by his own behavior, hopped on his horse and galloped away.

Chapter 13

False Start

"Care to join me?" Isaac asked.

Isaac sat at the kitchen table–his only friends a jug of whiskey and a glass. John walked into the kitchen and stopped in his tracks. He cocked his head when he saw the jug of whiskey but said nothing.

"What's the matter, don't feel like drinking?" asked Isaac.

John pulled up a chair, reached for a glass, and poured himself a shot. He focused on Isaac once again.

"I ain't never seen you drink before."

"You ain't never seen me drunk before," said Isaac, the play on words making him chuckle.

"What's going on little brother?"

"Well let's see. Rebecca called off the wedding, I spent the night with some lady named Fiona, and I think I slugged Edgar Putnam hard enough to break his jaw."

John dropped the glass he was holding, most of the liquid ending up in his lap.

"Goddammit, Isaac. You're starting to act like me."

"Not really, if I was you, I wouldn't give a shit."

Isaac, feeling sorry for himself, silently listed the grievances that swirled in his head. His dead father, Rebecca, Matt Burns, Charles Cunningham, the affair with Fiona, and this morning he attacked Mr. Putnam. Hardly the behavior of a good, Christian boy. The depressing tally prompted him to gulp another glass of whiskey. John, cleaning his mess, kept his eyes on Isaac the whole time.

"Are you all right? Is something botherin' you?"

"Yeah, I left my money at Rebecca's, and I really don't want to see her again. Can you get it for me?"

"Sure, sure, I can get it for you, first thing tomorrow."

John responded quickly, almost too quickly, Isaac thought. He was drunk but not that drunk.

"John, that's my money, don't be trying anything funny, because I'll kill you for sure, this time."

"I promise. No tricks. It'll be here tomorrow."

The two brothers talked for a while, taking turns with the jug when the other one's glass was empty. The booze did nothing to clear Isaac's head.

"I don't know what I'm going to do," said Isaac.

"There's always the army," said John.

"I couldn't kill a man if I wanted to. Don't you remember?"

"Oh, I remember. Boy, do I remember," said John.

They both laughed.

"Did you really slug Putnam?" asked John.

"Yup."

"Why?"

"Long story."

"How did you run into Fiona?"

"Another long story and I don't want to talk about it."

"Suit yourself."

There was a lull in the conversation. Isaac focused on his drink, chugged it down and slammed his glass on the table.

"My glass is empty."

When he reached for the jug, Isaac tipped to his right and gripped the table to steady himself. John watched as his brother crashed to the floor in a disheveled heap. With considerable effort, John walked, carried, and shoved his younger brother into the bedroom. The inebriated lad, his eyes already closed, muttered his gratitude.

"I still love you, John."

John left the farm early the next morning, his fake mission now underway.

With nowhere in particular to go, he wandered through the streets of Keeseville. Sherriff Bromley was watching from the window of his office; John tipped his hat. The lawman, his smoking pipe in one hand, appeared in the doorway and shouted.

"Where's your brother?"

"Home, nursing a hangover," said John.

"Mr. Putnam wants to press charges. What the hell happened?"

"He won't talk about it. But I'm proud of the boy; he's got a set of balls after all."

"Well, he's looking at a fifty dollar fine and maybe a week in the county lockup. Tell Isaac I wanna see him."

"Excuse me, Sheriff, I think you got company," said John, looking straight ahead.

Directly ahead of him, but on the boardwalk, was Mrs. Lobdell, unsmiling and walking with a purpose.

John pulled hard on the reins, turned his horse around, and galloped away.

"Good morning, Sheriff," said Mrs. Lobdell.

"Ma'am."

The sheriff removed his hat, motioned toward the door, and followed the lady into his office. When they were seated, the sheriff puffed hard on his pipe but it was cold. He put it to one side and leaned forward.

"What's on your mind, Mrs. Lobdell?"

Mrs. Lobdell related the details of her visit with John, just a few days ago. She swallowed hard on several occasions, desperate to maintain her composure.

"John took the money, and we called off the wedding. Sheriff, he said we could both go to jail."

Mrs. Lobdell dabbed at her eyes and shook her head.

"No one's going to jail," the sheriff announced.

"I'll ride out there today."

When John greeted the sheriff, the sack of coins was on the kitchen table.

"Have a seat," he said to the sheriff.

Bromley picked up a gold piece, inspected it, and tossed it in the open bag.

"Get your brother in here."

When Isaac came in from the barn, he spied the sack of money, scooped up the loose coins, and thanked his brother.

"Much obliged, John."

Bromley, not amused by John's chicanery, slammed his pipe on the table and glared at the older brother.

"You tried to blackmail Mrs. Lobdell and her daughter."

"Now Sheriff, that was just a misunderstanding. I was simply trying to get Isaac's money back."

"I think you got your days mixed up."

Bromley stood up and wagged his finger in John's direction.

"Now you listen to me, Boy, and you listen good."

"Mister Lobdell accidentally shot himself while cleaning his pistol. It's my word agin yours and ain't nobody gonna believe the town drunk."

John snorted, put his head down, and brushed an invisible breadcrumb from the tablecloth.

"What in tarnation are you two talking about?"

"I'm warning you, John. You leave them two women alone, you hear me?"

John blinked his acquiescence and nodded.

"Will someone please tell me what's going on?" Isaac pleaded."

The sheriff turned to Isaac but not to answer the boy's question.

"Mr. Putnam wants me to throw your ass in jail. You best get over there and apologize. Today," said the sheriff.

The sheriff let himself out, but not before he turned in the direction of his two law-breaking constituents.

"If I have to come out here again, one or the both of you are going to jail. Is that understood?"

"Yessir!"

The brothers spoke in perfect unison.

Isaac finished his chores, cleaned up, and trotted up the road, to Keeseville.

The boy, miffed and mystified that neither the sheriff nor his brother would explain their conversation about blackmail, contemplated a visit with the sheriff. Before that, however, he needed Mr. Putnam's forgiveness. The schoolmaster, still at the schoolhouse after hours, supervised empty desks and a room full of memories, not all pleasant.

"Mr. Putnam, may I come in?"

"You may."

"Mr. Putnam, you have the right to throw me in jail, and I wouldn't blame you if you did. I came here to apologize. You have been a great teacher and a good friend, and I'm truly sorry."

Isaac, choking with emotion, wanted to explain his behavior but chose not to, his embarrassment too much. Mr. Putnam, his jaw still tender and fingering a loose tooth, peered at the boy over wire-rimmed spectacles.

"You were my brightest pupil. Now you are my greatest disappointment."

Isaac's head slumped. A dozen blows from the schoolmaster's horsewhip produced less pain.

"I'm sorry, sir. I am very sorry."

"Go, and I hope never to see you again."

Isaac retreated, the path to his waiting horse, blurred by tears of shame.

"I apologized to Mr. Putnam."

Isaac stood in Sheriff Bromley's open doorway, afraid to enter and still unable to explain his behavior.

"Is he going to press charges?" asked Bromley.

"He said he never wants to see me again."

"Sit down, Isaac, there's something you oughta know."

Isaac shut the door and pulled up a chair. Bromley reached for his pipe and after minutes with a match and a series of puffs, spoke to Isaac through billowing clouds of aromatic smoke.

"Rebecca's stepfather raped her when she was twelve years old. She got a hold of his pistol and killed the bastard. Mrs. Lobdell tried to make it look like he was cleaning his gun, but the gun was in pieces. You can't shoot yourself if the gun's been disassembled. You understand what I'm saying?"

Isaac swallowed hard and nodded.

"I thought about hauling them in, but honestly, if that was my daughter, I would've shot the bastard myself."

"Your brother found out and blackmailed them. That's why she called off the wedding. They didn't want you to know the money was missing and they didn't want you to know about the shooting."

Isaac sat in his chair, stunned and speechless, the sheriff still talking.

"Isaac, are you listening?"

"Yes, sir. Sorry."

"Why did John give you the money? Why not keep it?" Bromley asked.

It required a few minutes for Isaac to collect his thoughts.

"I asked him to get my money from Rebecca, because I didn't want to see her again."

"But they had already given him the money. Now it makes sense. I could charge your brother, you know."

Isaac didn't care about his brother. Drowning in guilt and feeling pity for Rebecca, he got up to leave.

"Do you think she'd talk to me?" Isaac asked.

"You've got nothing to lose. And it would be a shame if the two of you split up. You do make a handsome couple."

Bromley smiled and blew a cloud of smoke.

Isaac rushed out the door and headed for Rebecca's

"I'll get it."

Mrs. Lobdell, in the middle of baking pies, heard the persistent knocking but could not respond.

"Rebecca."

The daughter hurried to the door, the sound of her footsteps acknowledging Mrs. Lobdell's request. She opened the door, smothered a cry with her hand, and stepped back.

"Rebecca, please, don't shut the door. Please!" said Isaac.

Mrs. Lobdell heard the boy's plea and appeared behind Rebecca, her apron and hands covered with flour, gripping a blue, checkered dishcloth as if it were a lifeline. Isaac didn't wait for a greeting.

"I know what happened to your stepfather. The sheriff told me."

Rebecca's face writhed in agony. She turned to her mother,

sobbing her relief, years of pain and suffering pouring from the child's eyes. Isaac stepped forward and pulled the hysterical girl into his arms. She cried into his shirt as he stroked her hair and patted her back.

"Rebecca, listen to me."

He cupped her face in his hands and used his thumbs to wipe her tears. Rebecca searched his eyes for the acceptance and understanding that had eluded her for so many years. Isaac didn't hesitate.

"Rebecca. What happened in the past doesn't matter to me. You are the only thing that truly matters. I love you. I will always love you. And I want you to be my wife. Please, Rebecca, I'm begging you. Will you marry me?"

She hid her teary face in his shirt, hugged him, and then pushed herself back, locking her eyes with his. She nodded, not once, but a whole series of nods, as rapidly as she could.

"Yes. Yes. I will marry you, Isaac Wells. I will marry you."

The young couple stood there in each other's arms, laughing and crying and hugging and kissing. Mrs. Lobdell used the dishtowel to paint her tear-stained cheeks, white with flour.

The Reverend Hagar presided over their wedding, Isaac and Rebecca insisting on a modest celebration.

A handful of friends and family gathered in the church hall to wish the happy couple a lifetime of health and happiness. Rebecca wore a plaid dress with a necklace neckline and long, puffy sleeves. The bodice, snug but not too tight, was separated from the skirt portion by a large, blue ribbon tied at the back. It would be the girl's best dress after the wedding, Victorian white being too impractical.

Isaac demanded John's acquiescence to a woman on the Wells' family farm. Given the circumstances of his attempt at blackmail, John faced prison or life on the farm with his brother's wife. The siblings calculated correctly that regular meals, a clean house, and help with the chores, would be a good thing. Rebecca grew up on a working farm and, except for an unnatural fear of bulls, voiced no objection to long days filled with hard work–the regimen at her mother's boarding house being just that. Cleaning, laundry services and preparing meals were not new to the new Mrs. Wells.

The sun had set when Isaac reached for his wife's hand and balanced the bride as she stepped off the buckboard. John, still at the church hall and likely spending the night in Keeseville, remained behind. Isaac relished the thought of his brother's absence, on that night in particular.

The groom donned a clean nightshirt and waited patiently under the covers for his new bride to finish her evening rituals. She lingered over her long, red hair, brushing her locks for what seemed to Isaac an extraordinarily long while. He blew out the flame in the oil lamp as she climbed into the marital bed.

He reached for her, held her tight, and smiled to himself, because his would-be lover was trembling. He pulled her face toward his, and they kissed. Isaac tugged at her nightdress, and she instinctively captured his hand, unwilling to let the exploration go any further. He waited, kissed her several times, the passion in his loins stirring, and again, triggered the same response.

"Rebecca, it's all right."

"I can't," she sobbed.

Puzzled and frustrated, he rolled onto his back and stared into the darkness. He recalled the sins of her stepfather and with great effort, smothered his own carnal desires.

"Rebecca, there's no hurry, maybe tomorrow."

She turned away from him, assumed a fetal position, and drifted off to a restless sleep.

Rebecca worked hard to please her husband, cleaning the house, cooking the meals, washing the clothes, feeding the small animals, and collecting the eggs. As expected, she refused to deal with the monstrous bull, deathly afraid of his long-curved horns and intimidated by his size and strength. Feeding him, much less moving him from pasture to pasture, would be the purview of her husband, his brother, or the hired hand.

She also refused to accommodate her husband in their bedroom. Despite Isaac's protests, several of them shouted, the virgin bride would not consummate their marriage. Isaac withdrew into his chores, the summer months being the busiest of times on their upstate, New York farm. His resentment and frustration grew by the day.

After a quiet lunch of cold chicken and boiled potatoes, Rebecca sensed his anger and dared to broach the subject.

"Do you hate me?" she asked.

"I married you, didn't I?"

"I want to be a good wife to you, Isaac, really I do."

"Then start acting like a good wife."

Angrier now than before, Isaac stood up, knocking his chair to the floor and sliding it into the doorway. He kicked hard, sending the wooden chair across the room, just missing Rebecca and causing her to step back in fear.

"I'm sorry, Isaac. I'm sorry," she sobbed.

Isaac refused to acknowledge her apologies and left.

She watched through the window as he saddled his horse and rode off in a cloud of dust.

Chapter 14

Lovers

Isaac wandered into the Ausable House, angry and frustrated with his new bride.

No beer this time, just a strong coffee. The boy, staring into space, wondered how and why his life became such a nightmare. His marriage to Rebecca, a salve for losing his father and dear friends, added to the boy's woes. The new beginning he anticipated became a bitter disappointment, his dream, a nightmare, almost as soon as it began. The boy's marriage, obviously a tragic mistake, could not be saved, he thought. Despite her best intentions, the broken girl could not recover from her gaping wounds.

"You look like someone I know."

Isaac looked up and grinned.

"Fiona, it's so nice to see you again. Can you sit for a while?"

She greeted him with a kiss on the forehead, and they conversed like two old friends. She interrupted Isaac in the middle of his narrative about Matt Burns.

"Excuse me."

As Issac watched, Fiona ran to the open door, leaned over the porch railing and wretched into the gutter. She wiped her face with a yellow hanky, straightened her dress, and returned to the table.

"Fiona, you're white as a sheet. Shall I bring you to Doc McLean's"

"The morning sickness is just a symptom, I know what the problem is," she said.

The woman smiled and then swallowed hard, in an effort to suppress her nausea.

"Are you?" he asked.

"With child," she finished his question.

Isaac, oblivious to the implications of her condition, rattled on about his own desire for children, boys in particular, and how he wanted children with Rebecca, but she seemed unwilling. Isaac debated whether or not he should share the details of his strained marriage, but the blank stare on Fiona's face startled him into silence. He studied her face; she looked away.

"Fiona. Look at me. Am I the father?"

Fiona frowned, shook her head no, and reassured her married ex-lover.

"No, Isaac. He has no idea. The baby is my responsibility."

Fiona answered a question he didn't ask. She made a distinction without a difference. Isaac didn't notice, his youthful naïvetè blinding him to the truth.

"I have to go now," she announced, rising to her feet and clearing her throat.

Isaac noticed that the strong, exuberant, and self-confident woman he met just once before, now looked like a scared kitten, sickly and unsure as to where she should go next.

"How are you going to support yourself. What are you going to do?"

Before she could respond, Isaac reached into his pocket and pressed a few coins into her hands. She objected.

"No, I can't take your money."

"Fiona, look at me."

She smiled her acceptance and left him standing there.

In time, Isaac stopped pressuring his wife for the intimacy he desired.

He resigned himself to living with Rebecca as if cohabitating with his sister. He watched her, working hard from sun up to sundown. Isaac viewed her actions as a self-inflicted penance for Rebecca's sins of omission. But her apology for their platonic relationship had no effect. The young man remained angry and frustrated.

Isaac, now making regular trips into the village and always with a handful of coins for Fiona, adjusted to his new life as best he could. Fiona, three months into her pregnancy, and grateful for the financial support, refused to discuss the child's paternity. Isaac thought of quietly divorcing his wife but dismissed the idea, worried more about embarrassing Rebecca then his own miserable existence. He fantasized about Fiona, imagining that they were in each other's arms once again. The impossible delusion and his lust for Fiona did not spur him to break his marital vows. Instead, he suffered.

When the 'dog-days of August' arrived, tempers flared.

"Going into town?"

Rebecca, standing in the bedroom door, startled her husband as he removed coins from the sack which used to contain their dreams.

"Yes"

"You got supplies last week. What's the money for?"

"If you must know, it's for a friend."

"Is your friend's name, Fiona?"

Isaac sat on the edge of the bed, studying the coins in his hand, head drooping.

"Yes," he said.

"John said the two of you were lovers."

Isaac winced. Fiona persisted.

"Is it true?"

"Once, just before you and I got married."

Isaac studied the wallpaper, Rebecca focused on her husband, chewing on her nails and pulling at her hair.

"Do you love her?"

Isaac, dumped half of the coins onto the bed, shoving the sack with the remainder into his haversack. He added a few articles of clothing and a book.

"I'm not sleeping with her if that's what you mean."

"That's not what I asked."

"Rebecca, I married you, not Fiona. I loved you then, and I love you now. But this isn't working, and I can't do it anymore. Do you understand? I'm leaving, Rebecca, I don't want to, but I have to. What happened years ago is not your fault. But it's not my fault either."

He brushed past Rebecca on his way out the door. She didn't stop him. There were no tears in her eyes.

Isaac could not recall his ride from the farmhouse to the Ausable House. He left the balance of the money for Fiona, a short note in the sack, trusting the Negro servant to do as he was told. Isaac's journey did not end in Keeseville, his trip to Plattsburgh requiring hours more. But Isaac was on a mission. Blurry eyed and stiff from his journey, the young man walked awkwardly into the stone building known as the barracks. An older man, in blue, sat at a makeshift desk comprising two barrels and several rough-cut boards.

"May I help you?" the soldier asked.

"Yes. My name is Isaac Wells, and I'd like to enlist."

John noticed his little brother's absence.

"What do you mean, he left?"

John neither liked what he heard from Rebecca nor did he understand it.

"Just what I said. He took half of the money, too."

"Why did he leave? It's not that Fiona girl is it?"

"No, it's not her. It's me."

"You just got married. What in tarnation is going on?"

Rebecca started crying, shook her head, and stumbled to her room. John complained to the kitchen walls.

"Great. I'm gonna get stuck with all his chores."

John swung by the Widow Burns' place before he left for Keeseville. Mrs. Burns had not seen Isaac in days. John's next stop was the Ausable House. Fiona refused to open the door, until John explained that his little brother was missing.

"Isaac is missing?"

"That's what I've been trying to tell you, Fiona."

"I haven't seen him, but he did."

"He did what?"

Fiona hesitated.

"What did he do?"

"He left me some money. I'm in a family way. I think he felt sorry for me."

"Oh, that's really nice of him. I'm going to pay to have his chores done, but you get the money."

John huffed and headed over to Mrs. Lobdell's boarding house.

"Mr. Wells, you are not welcome here," she said.

John was standing in the doorway and used his foot to stop Mrs. Lobdell from shutting the door in his face.

"Isaac is missing. Have you seen him?"

She explained that neither Isaac nor Rebecca had been to the boarding house in several weeks.

"The Reverend Hagar was asking about them this past Sunday. They haven't attended services, since they got married," she reported.

John shook his head, didn't bother to say thank you or goodbye, and headed to the schoolhouse. Putnam was tidying up, his students on their way out. John didn't bother with the amenities.

"I'm looking for Isaac, have you seen him?"

"No, I have not, nor do I want to."

John smiled.

"How's your jaw?"

He left before the schoolmaster could respond.

John stopped at the sheriff's office, next.

"Have you seen my little brother?"

"No," said Bromley, chugging on his pipe. "What's going on?"

"He told his brand-new wife that he was leaving her. If he doesn't show up pretty soon, I'm going to have to get me another hired hand," said John.

"Have you checked the Ausable House?"

"I've checked everywhere, the Ausable House, the boarding house, the school, Widow Burns' place, everywhere. He's gone like a fart in the wind. That ain't like Isaac, him being everyone's darling, little angel."

"I can see how much you miss him." said the sheriff.

John rolled his eyes and headed toward the door.

"Thanks for nothing."

Chapter 15

Enlisted

Isaac's first night at the barracks did not go as he expected.

Straw on the barracks floor made for a decent night's sleep, but nobody slept. Non-stop joking, fooling around, and bragging made sleep impossible. The recruits practiced their marching for most of the next morning, despite the absence of guns and uniforms. A constant flow of new enlistees, most looking younger than the minimum requirement of eighteen years, interrupted the boredom. Physical exams were the exception, not the rule, and only obvious maladies prevented a recruit from serving. Isaac was introduced to many of the recruits, and was surprised to meet lawyers, merchants, farmers, college men, mechanics, store clerks, and even a doctor.

In the days that followed, many recruits received visits or packages of foodstuff and supplies from friends, neighbors, and loved ones. But not Isaac. No one knew he was there.

"Want some?"

The blonde-haired kid caught Isaac sitting on the front stoop of the barracks and offered to share some of his cider cakes.

"My mom made 'em. Try one. They're really good."

Isaac grabbed one and with his mouth full mumbled his thanks. "Much obliged."

"Thaddeus Wilkins, but everybody calls me Thad."

The kid stuck his hand out, Isaac returned the gesture and forced a smile.

"Isaac, Isaac Wells."

"Ain't your folks sent you nothin?" the boy asked.

"Not yet."

"Where you from?"

"Keeseville."

"I'm from Elizabethtown. We're pretneer neighbors."

Isaac smiled and turned down another cider cake with a shake of his head.

"I hope we get our uniforms before we leave," said Thad.

"We leaving soon?"

"We take the steamer to Whitehall on the first of September. The sarge told me."

"That's the end of this week. You sure?" asked Isaac.

"Yup, the 118th Regiment is off to war," said Wilkins, as he trotted off to the parade grounds.

Isaac went in search of pencil and paper.

As the 118th, dubbed the Adirondack Regiment, prepared to leave, Isaac struggled to put into words the pain and suffering that prompted him to enlist. His vowed that his first letter to home would be his only letter.

Rebecca,

I have enlisted in the army and know not when, or even if, I shall return. Please forgive me for having abandoned you in our time of need. It is a poor husband who professes his love but is too weak to withstand its obligations. I pray that time will heal the wounds from which you suffer and soothe the injuries which I too have inflicted upon your person.

Yours,

Isaac Wells, 118th Rgmt.

Isaac swallowed hard, folded his letter, placed it in the envelope, and carried it to the clerk in charge of such matters.

"I don't have a stamp," said Isaac.

"Write 'Soldiers Letter' on the envelope. Whoever gets it pays for the postage," said the clerk.

Isaac did as he was told, wondering to himself if Rebecca or John would be willing to pay the three cents.

The Adirondack Regiment received its uniforms on the day before it left Plattsburgh.

Isaac and his colleagues marched to their waiting steamboat in a cold, drizzling rain. The streets of Plattsburgh, lined with well-wishers, friends, and loved ones, echoed with the sound of hundreds of feet hitting the hardscrabble surface. The somber procession, randomly interrupted by a friend's shouted farewell, brought many of the on-lookers to tears. Mostly, it was the steady rain and muted sobs of family members, that serenaded the long, blue line of soldiers as they marched off to war.

Isaac's previous excursion to Whitehall bore little resemblance to the dreary sojourn which lay ahead of him. Regimental Officers were assigned to the handful of onboard staterooms, everyone else was forced to stand, sit, or sleep on the steamboat's open-air deck. Although the sun was setting, soldiers too excited or too uncomfortable to sleep, strained to spot familiar landmarks on Lake Champlain's western shore. A fleeting glance of a home, barn, or field triggered a war hoop, a knowing smile or even, the occasional tear. No one referred to the fact that, for some men, such things would never be seen again.

They reached Whitehall early the next day, on the morning of September second. A long train of boxcars, with a few platform cars mixed in, waited for its soggy cargo. The soldiers felt like cattle, officers struggling to pack too many men into too few box cars, and then relenting when it became obvious that more cars were needed. Some soldiers used cordwood, pilfered from a nearby pile, to pound the sides off their box cars, accomplishing a steady source of fresh air and the occasional panoramic view. The Rensselaer and Saratoga railcars would arrive in Albany with some obvious "wounds," all of it from "friendly fire."

The summer sun shone on the troops when they made their first stop en route to Albany, at Saratoga Springs. The shiny, gold-colored buttons on their new uniforms became the coin of the realm when the recruits realized that, for a single button, a young maiden would embrace and kiss the warrior goodbye and good luck. Flowers, fruit, and confections were also given to the troops and many a soldier gave and received personal effects, personal addresses, and some very personal promises.

At noon, the regiment arrived in Albany. After a fine lunch, hosted by the Adjutant's mother, the soldiers crossed the Hudson and bordered yet another train, this time for New York City. The widespread complaint that soldiers were transported like cattle became obvious, as the train out of Albany, previously used for the transport of farm animals, contained large quantities of smelly evidence. When the train pulled into New York City well past midnight, the troops marched to City Hall Park and took up residence in temporary barracks, constructed for their arrival. The high, iron fence which surrounded the park separated the soldiers from unwanted visitors and trespassers. After a quiet and uneventful night, during which most troops slept soundly, the regiment woke up to the noise of New York City and the vision of dozens of hucksters peddling their wares to any soldier who dared to approach the wrought iron barrier. Knives, pistols, trinkets, and almost anything edible could be purchased by the soldiers. Eventually, the street merchants were chased off by the military guard, after both sides complained of being cheated.

When, in the afternoon, Tom Thumb, of P. T. Barnum fame, appeared at the museum across the street a wave of excitement rushed through the regiment. Hundreds of soldiers ran the gate but dutifully returned in time for the march to Broadway and their next steamer. By morning, the regiment arrived in Philadelphia and, it being a hot day, were all too happy to accept a wagon load of watermelons donated to the troops by a traveling merchant. By late afternoon, the reason for the donation became obvious, when hundreds of men doubled over in pain, vomited and struggled with violent gastrointestinal eruptions. Isaac, who never liked the taste of watermelons, considered himself fortunate not to have been affected.

Another train, this one consisting mostly of platform cars, brought the troops to Baltimore. In that city, the crowds were not so friendly and the soldiers, still without their weapons or gear, understandably nervous. A whole night waiting for another train, this one to Harpers Ferry, meant that most men slept on sidewalks or propped up against a nearby building. The morning sun shone on the men in more ways than one, when on the next day their long-awaited Enfield rifles arrived, with tents, camping equipment, and various accoutrements.

At the last moment, their orders to proceed to Harpers Ferry countermanded, the regiment marched to the Thomas Viaduct. The only train to Washington from the North passed through this junction, rendering it a strategic location which required constant guard against cavalry and unexpected raids.

Later, Isaac and his colleagues received word that Stonewall Jackson captured the Union garrison at Harpers Ferry. But for their last-minute change in orders, members of the Adirondack Regiment might well have joined Jackson's twelve thousand prisoners of war.

A few days later, the 118th was bombarded by the noise of large cannon being fired in the bloody battle at Antietam, just a few miles away. Everyone breathed easier after learning that Lee's forces retreated, and the Viaduct was safe, once again.

Chapter 16

The Unknown

"You have a letter from Isaac. Cost me three cents," said John.

Rebecca's heart skipped a beat as she abandoned her shawl at the door and rushed to the kitchen table.

"It's been opened," she said, scowling at her brother-in-law.

"It's just a love letter. He didn't even ask about me or the farm," said John.

Rebecca clutched the note to her chest and grabbed her wrap, bolted out the door, glaring at John as she left. She refused to read it until she found the shade of a large tree, on the side of the road, a short distance from the family farm. Rebecca mouthed the words, first to herself and then out loud, over and over again. When tears splashed onto the paper, she panicked and took great pains to dab the letter dry, a desperate attempt to erase the evidence of her heartbreak and preserve the record of her husband's love.

"News from Isaac?"

Rebecca recognized the voice and outline of Widow Burns. The older woman stood, with her back to the sun, gazing at the sorrowful sight beneath the large oak tree.

"He doesn't love me anymore," Rebecca said, her sobs giving way to sniffles and a sad look.

"Why wouldn't he love such a beautiful girl?" asked Mrs. Burns.

Rebecca could think of at least one reason, but instead, she blurted the news.

"He enlisted. My husband is off to war."

The young bride, overcome with the despair once again, wept violently and reached for her neighbor. Mrs. Burns sat beside her, cradling the girl while stroking Rebecca's beautiful, red hair. The girl sobbed once more and then caught a deep breath. The old woman's presence seemed to have a calming influence. Without warning, Rebecca bolted upright and studied Mrs. Burn's face.

"You lost your son to this miserable war, and here I am crying on your shoulder. I'm so sorry, Mrs. Burns, I'm so sorry."

The widow smiled, dabbing quickly at the tear which escaped from one eye and rolled down her tanned and wrinkled check.

"It's all right, Honey, I'm just about out of tears for my Matthew. Let's worry about Isaac instead."

"You can read it if you want to," Rebecca said, certain that the widow would have questions, questions Rebecca was eager to answer.

Mrs. Burns studied the soldier's letter for some time.

"Wounds? Injuries? Is there something wrong? Are you hurt?"

Rebecca confided in her kindly neighbor, Mrs. Burns, who was forced to hush her own shocked response to Rebecca's tale of horror.

"Isaac knows what happened to me, the sheriff knows, and John overheard a conversation with my mother and me. But I don't care about that."

Rebecca captured Mrs. Burns stare.

"Isaac and I may be married, but we are not yet husband and wife."

Mrs. Burns eyes grew wide, Rebecca did not flinch.

"I want to but I can't."

The aging widow blushed but recovered.

"Oh, you poor girl. You poor, little girl."

There were no more tears, Rebecca was numb and uncertain as to what she should do next. Mrs. Burns encouraged Rebecca to write back, instructing her to send the letters to Isaac in care of the Plattsburgh barracks where, presumably, they would know the whereabouts of the 118th Regiment.

"I can't tell you what to write, Honey, but I know he would be happy to hear from you. He needs to hear from you. War changes a man. And if the good Lord is willing to bring him home, the rest will work out. I'm sure of it," said the old woman.

The widow and the young bride rose from their hiding place in the shade and embraced each other in the warm glow of a sunlit sky.

Fiona rested on the landing, a single flight of stairs between her and the Ausable House lobby.

She cursed her third-floor room and reached for the railing, as the hallway began to spin. The stairs moved, her legs wobbled, and she struggled to maintain her balance. She felt herself go forward and then tumbled helplessly into a black abyss.

"Can you hear me?"

Fiona blinked her eyes and forced them to focus on the elderly man standing by the bedside. She did not recognize him or the room where she lay. This was not the Ausable House, she thought.

"I'm Doc McLean. You took a bad fall, ma'am. No broken bones but I am worried about the baby."

Fiona's eyes grew wide, she grabbed the man by his arm and attempted to pull herself into a sitting position.

"Don't get up; you need to lay still."

"The baby. Is he, all right?"

"I think the baby is fine, but I have to ask. How do you know it's a boy?"

Fiona exhaled, the panic draining from her face.

"I just know," she said. "I just know."

"You need to stay off your feet as much as you can, until the baby is born."

"But I live at the Ausable House."

"I know where you live, Fiona. I'm going to ask Mrs. Lobdell at the boarding house if she'll put you up. Can you afford to pay her?"

"Yes, but."

"Get some rest; I'll be back."

Fiona tried to explain but her eyes fluttered from exhaustion, and she fell into a deep sleep.

Mrs. Lobdell knew Fiona by sight and by reputation.

"Doctor McLean, I will not provide room and board for a woman of ill repute."

"She's with child, Mrs. Lobdell. Surely, as a Christian woman, you can understand my predicament. She has the money to pay you."

"Yes, I'm sure she does, and we both know how she earned it."

"Please, Mrs. Lobdell, her baby could be in danger."

The old woman, tempted to shut the door in Doc McLean's face, recalled his almost daily visits with Abraham Wells. McLean was an honorable man and a good doctor. She shook her head and frowned her reluctant approval.

"I have a spare room on the first floor."

"She's resting now. I'll have some of the men bring her over, later this afternoon."

McLean thanked the woman, tipped his hat, and stepped off the porch. Mrs. Lobdell had just enough time to prepare the downstairs guestroom when the knock on her front door signaled Fiona's arrival. The patient, in and out of consciousness, felt the effects of McLean's prescriptions. Fiona followed Mrs. Lobdell with her eyes, as the older woman hustled around the room and prepared for her newest guest. Fiona whispered a 'thank you' as Lobdell turned in the patient's direction.

"I'll make you a cup of tea with some fresh bread, after you have rested."

"Who goes there?"

Isaac, serving guard duty, nervously walked his post. Tensions in the camp were extremely high, given the Union's bloody defeat at Harpers Ferry and their near-loss at Antietam, just down the road. When the visitor responded with the correct countersign, Isaac waived him forward but flinched when the hammer on the Enfield rifle pinned his thumb to the percussion cap. Earlier, the novice soldier cocked his weapon in contemplation of an intruder. But when the stranger approached the amateur soldier, Isaac forgot that his index finger was resting on the trigger. He squeezed without thinking. Nerves. The fellow soldier went on his merry way knowing not how close he came to being shot in the chest. Isaac required minutes of deep breathing before his panic subsided and he was able to resume his lonely post, this time with an uncocked rifle.

Just weeks ago, another sentry accidentally discharged his weapon into the smokestack of a waiting train. The ricochet killed the Baltimore engineer, and the soldier was carted off to stand trial. The local press, unsympathetic to the Union cause, pushed for a trial by jury and Isaac's brother-in-arms stood convicted of manslaughter. But for a governor's pardon, this soldier faced execution for his accidental shooting.

On September 13, the 118th Regiment was moved to a new camp, just a mile away. Camp Wool, on a low-lying wetland near the Potomac, did not welcome its newest inhabitants. Isaac marched, stood, lay, and sat in the pest-filled muck, with either stifling heat or a cold, blowing wind to keep him company.

His suffering would continue.

"You have typhoid."

Isaac questioned the doctor with glassy eyes, refusing to believe what he had heard. He shook his head, disagreeing with the diagnosis but unable to voice his objections to a prognosis which included the possibility of death.

"Whiskey, twice a day, cold compresses, and weak coffee."

A nearby orderly made a note of the doctor's instructions, and both went on to another patient in the temporary hospital, which a few months ago, operated as a functioning barn. Isaac thought back to his time in the swamp, recalling the hours he spent there, often immersed in a filthy muck. Several alerts, most two to three days in length, required the troops to maintain a defensive perimeter, regardless of conditions. Dozens of soldiers contracted the fever, extreme fatigue, or all three. Isaac, too weak to rise from his cot, remained in the barn for days. After several weeks, his fever broke, and he could digest small amounts of food and drink. He made slow but steady progress, eventually visiting the other patients, and offering to read their letters from home or write a response, many too weak to do either. Isaac's boredom and a strong suggestion from his corporal prompted the otherwise altruistic visits. He also made the short trek to the post hospital, occupied by the most seriously ill of his comrades. Several men died from their illness and Isaac, being an educated recruit, received orders from his corporal to write to the victims' families. Isaac, although grateful for the continued opportunity to rest and recover, despised the assignment, because his missives brought so much pain and suffering to the folks back home.

He learned of his next assignment when he returned to the 118th. The troops moved a short distance across the Potomac to Fort Ethan Allen, just above Washington DC. Isaac's regiment, part of a larger force, was being tasked with the job of protecting the nation's capital city. The dome of the Capitol building, still under construction and surrounded by scaffolding, dominated the landscape. Fort Ethan Allen, almost as new, consisted of earthen works fortifications. The star-shaped bastion garrisoned more than a thousand men plus artillery pieces.

Isaac, although pleased with his new accommodations, commiserated with his fellow soldiers about the paymaster. This man offered no reasonable explanation for his lack of funds. Three weeks of no pay made the men irritable and angry. The camp sutler, a civilian merchant that hung with the regiment, offered to loan the men an advance, exacting a healthy fee for doing so. Some of the men, desperate for their regular allotment of thirteen dollars per month, took advantage of the offer. Isaac calculated that if the scoundrel was prepared to loan that much money to so many men, the paymaster would soon arrive.

He did. Several days later.

Chapter 17

A Helping Hand

"I am an unwanted guest."

Fiona dared to confront Mrs. Lobdell, as the old woman scurried about the bedchamber folding clothes, straightening the quilt and opening the curtains. Mrs. Lobdell stopped, gazed out the window and then turned.

"Where is the father?" she demanded.

Fiona hesitated, while Mrs. Lobdell stood there, arms folded across her chest and staring down at her unwanted boarder. Fiona knew that Isaac enlisted, thanks to the short note in his sack of coins, now committed to her memory.

Fiona, I have enlisted and will not see you again.
Yours truly, Isaac Wells

"I don't know."

Fiona spoke in a whisper; her blank stare focused on the large maple tree which decorated the view from her window. The leaves swayed gently in the breeze as Fiona's thoughts drifted to her lover. Mrs. Lobdell ruined Fiona's vision with a single sentence.

"You'll never see him again."

The old woman reached for Fiona's wooden breakfast tray and huffed her way through the open door. The unborn child in her womb leapt, as Fiona lay back on her pillow. It occurred to the pregnant woman that neither Mrs. Lobdell nor her daughter knew that Isaac fathered her unborn child. She wanted to keep it that way.

But Fiona dreamed about a letter from Isaac. Proof that he loved her, as much as she loved him. War changes a man, she thought. Perhaps she could become more than his one-time lover. A letter to her man in blue might trigger a response, she thought. But how? Pen and paper would be easy enough. Posting a letter to a married man would raise eyebrows, if not suspicions.

Fiona smiled. She had a plan.

"Where are you going?"

Isaac was watching Thad Stevens, the boy from Elizabethtown, as he slammed his few belongings into a haversack and turned to leave.

"I aim to see Mr. Lincoln."

Isaac, sitting on the edge of the cot, rose and grabbed his friend by the shoulders.

"Thad, you can't walk into the White House and see the President of the United States.

"My father is dying, and the lieutenant doesn't give a damn. I don't care what he says, I'm gonna get my furlough, and I intend to see my old man before he dies."

Stevens was adamant and unwilling to change his mind despite Isaac's pleas. Isaac was sympathetic, temporarily immersed in the memories of his own father's death.

"I'll go with you; I still owe you for the cider cakes."

Both men were somber as they confronted the afternoon chill of Washington in October. It took the pair less than an hour to reach the White House and not surprisingly, a large man in blue stopped the naïve boy from Elizabethtown.

"Where are you going, Son?"

Thad explained his mission to the guard. The sentry shook his head violently. "Unless Mr. Lincoln is expecting you, this is as far as you go." The sentry stood not fifty yards from the Executive Mansion's main entrance.

"Come on, Thad, let's go," said Isaac, tugging at his friend's elbow.

"I'm not going anywhere."

Thad raised his voice, explaining again the need to see his dying father as soon as possible.

"Move on, Soldier, you're not going to see the president."

A pushing match ensued and more yelling.

Thad screamed.

"You can't prevent me from seeing the president. I see him now."

The raw recruit spied the tall, thin figure, as the president approached the mansion's exit. The clamor prompted Lincoln to look up and then walk over to investigate the ruckus. Thad wasted no time; the president listened in silence. Thad came up for air after one last plea.

"Mr. President, I do so want to see my father again, before he dies."

"Of course, you do," said Lincoln. "Walk with me; I am on my way to the war department."

Isaac walked behind the two men but within earshot. The president asked Stevens his father's age, if his mother was still living, whether he had siblings and other kindly questions. In time, the soldier and his commander-in-chief disappeared behind a set of heavily-guarded doors. Moments later, Stevens emerged, tears in his eyes, but smiling broadly.

"I am all broken up by that great man's kindness to me. Me, only a private, among thousands."

Stevens took the next day's train on a ten-day furlough, arriving home a full two days before his father passed away. The grieving but grateful soldier returned to Washington the day before his furlough expired.

Isaac, more enamored now with his president than before, listened to the details of Thad's visit as they munched on some freshly baked cider muffins.

Doc McLean looked forward to his first house call, this early November morning.

He liked Fiona Dunham and enjoyed her company, despite her checkered past. Now completing her sixth month, McLean thought it best to check on both her and the baby.

"Most women in your condition would have no reason to smile," Doc McLean commented while listening to Fiona's heart.

"Oh, I've got lots of things to complain about, Doc, but it doesn't seem to make a difference, so why bother," said Fiona, still smiling.

The doctor grinned and nodded his agreement. He paused and adopted a more serious tone.

"I'm going to reach under your nightdress, now," he said.

He maintained eye contact with his patient or stared at the wall, conducting his examination entirely by touch. He finished, wiping his bare hand on a nearby towel.

"Everything seems fine. Are you having any troubles?" he asked.

"He kicks a lot," Fiona replied.

"A bit early for that, in my opinion . . . for a boy or a girl," said McLean, indulging the woman's desire for a boy.

"It's a boy, trust me."

As the doctor packed his things and reached for his coat, Fiona tossed a letter into his black leather satchel. He noticed.

"Would you deliver it to the post office?" she asked.

"Sure thing. It's on the way to my next house call."

"Thank you, Doc."

Rebecca hummed as she entered her mother's boarding house, the response to Isaac's letter, was now posted and professed her love, now more than ever.

She also collected letters to Isaac from Mrs. Burns and Mr. Putnam. Her soldier-husband would not be without word from home.

"Momma, I sure could use a spot of tea. Oh, hello."

Rebecca stopped short when she noticed a woman through the open door of the downstairs bedchamber.

"Momma doesn't usually rent this room out to boarders."

"Mrs. Lobdell has been very kind," said Fiona.

"I'm Rebecca, Mrs. Lobdell is my mother."

Rebecca curtsied ever so slightly to the older, bedridden woman. Fiona chose not to introduce herself. Rebecca insisted.

"I'm sorry, what is your name?"

Fiona hesitated, took a deep breath, and then exhaled.

"My name is Fiona Dunham."

Rebecca stared at the woman, her mind racing and then recalling and then recoiling.

"Why are you here?" she demanded.

"The doctor said I needed bedrest. Your mother was kind enough to rent me a room. It's temporary of course."

"Are you sick?"

"No."

Fiona's response inflamed the virgin bride.

"Isaac Wells is my husband, and we are happily married," said Rebecca, a defensive tone in her shaky voice. Fiona spoke softly.

"I understand."

"Good day, Miss Dunham."

Rebecca, her disgust obvious, glared and then bustled down the hallway in search of her mother. Mrs. Lobdell, replacing sheets in an upstairs bedchamber, greeted her daughter.

"Good morning, Sweetheart."

"Mother, how could you do such a thing?"

"I assume you are referring to our downstairs guest."

"You must ask her to leave, immediately."

"Listen to me, Child. I know what kind of woman she is, but Doctor McLean was desperate, and I just couldn't refuse him."

"She doesn't look sick to me, what's wrong with her?"

"Rebecca, she is in a family way, I can't very well kick her into the street, now can I?"

Rebecca reached for the bedpost to steady herself and smothered an audible gasp with her other hand. The color drained from her face, and she fixed her gaze on the hardwood floor.

"Are you feeling poorly?" asked Mrs. Lobdell.

Rebecca's head jerked up, she cleared her throat and used her hands to brush back her hair, pinned neatly into a bun. She forced herself to feign an outward calm.

"I'm fine, Momma, it's much too stuffy up here, I must go. Where is that letter to Isaac?"

"What's your problem?"

John Wells caught Rebecca crying, the girl clinging to her coffee cup but leaving the liquid unmolested.

"I'm fine," she announced.

John threw a piece of cordwood into the buck stove, a small gesture given the cold, November wind whistling through the farmhouse.

"Wanna talk about it?" asked John, as he fell into the chair nearest Rebecca.

"I can't."

John reached for his sister-in-law's hands, holding them in his own. Rebecca pulled back.

"Aw come on, Rebecca, I'm not the enemy. Isaac's gone, and we have to face the fact that he may never come back. We have to stick together."

John grabbed her hands again and caressed her fingers. Rebecca, distracted by his awful suggestion, did nothing to discourage the man's clumsy advance. He pulled her hands closer and pressed his lips to her palms. Rebecca jolted from her train of horrible thought, yanked her hands, tipped the coffee cup, and spilled its contents onto her lap. She jumped to her feet, angry and wet.

"What are you doing?"

John laughed at the woman, scorn in his eyes.

"You'll come around. As soon as you realize that your sweetheart ain't never coming back."

He moved to the parlor, parked himself in the old man's rocking chair, and reached for the hunting knife. Satisfied with himself, John pulled the blade over the whetstone, as if preparing to carve a Christmas turkey.

Chapter 18
Suffering

"Mail call."

Isaac hopped off his cot. No one in the regiment had received even a single letter from friends or family, since the time of their enlistment more than three months ago. He grabbed the first letter from the corporal's hand and noticed that it was from his former schoolmaster, Mr. Putnam. The young soldier stared at the envelope in disbelief and shock. Before he could open the envelope, another shout from the officer.

"Wells."

Mrs. Lobdell and Mrs. Burns had also taken the time to write. The corporal had but a handful of letters remaining, Isaac turned toward his bunk, sad and discouraged.

"Wells."

The boy turned and pushed his way through the mob of expectant soldiers.

"Here, here," he shouted.

"Was there anyone back home who did not write to you?' asked the grinning corporal.

Isaac recognized the handwriting and forced himself to wait until he was in the semi-privacy of his own bunk. Even then, he studied her penmanship and savored the joy of a letter from the woman he loved. He opened the envelope with great care, not wanting to damage its contents in any way.

Dear husband,

I have received yours of the 19th and thank the Lord Almighty that you are safe and in good health. I must reject your apology and beg of you to accept my own. It is your sorrowful wife who has brought so much heartache into this marriage and I pray that you will forgive me for my many weaknesses. I pray also that you will return to our home unharmed and in good health. It is my greatest prayer however that you will, once again, bestow on me the honor of being

Your loving wife,
Rebecca

At that moment, Isaac questioned his decision to leave home and enlist. He wondered if and how he would survive the three years of his enlistment. He quickly opened the remaining letters, smiling at Mrs. Burns' promise of an apple pie when he returned and laughing out loud when Mrs. Lobdell expressed her annoyance that the rocking chairs on her porch were now perpetually empty. The letter from his former schoolmaster was a reminder that law school was still an option.

Still, the recruit could not bring himself to write to any of his friends back home, particularly, his wife.

"I need your help."

Rebecca, busy in the kitchen when John appeared at the front door, glared at her brother-in-law and was still angry about his unwanted approach of just one week ago.

"Shut the door, it's freezing out there," she replied.

"It's past time we move the bull into the barn. I'm all alone today."

"Where's Lucas?"

Lucas was the teenager that John had hired shortly after buying the tavern. He was a hard-working lad, painfully shy, and kept to himself, mostly.

"Needed the day off. Said his momma needed him to fix a leaky roof."

"I've told you before; I'm not going anywhere near that thing."

John laughed.

"Once I get the rope through his nose ring, he'll be fine. All you gotta do is drive him to the corner of the pasture. I'm the one who's gonna get hurt."

Rebecca shook her head, her disapproval, obvious.

"You can even have the pitchfork, he hates the pitchfork," said John

Rebecca sighed loudly, reached for her wraps plus an old coat and walked behind her brother-in-law to the nearby pasture. The bull did as he was urged, and John threaded the thick rope on his first attempt. The oversized monster seemed eager to reach the warmth of the barn. Rebecca, bringing up the rear in the slow-moving parade of man, beast, and woman, entered the aisle in the rundown barn. It could have been a mouse or perhaps a stray cat, but something startled the massive beast. Rebecca's eyes grew wide when the monster bull, without warning, took a few steps back, his hooves slipping in the frozen muck. She moved to her right but not quick enough. The bull's right flank sent the woman sprawling, and one of his hooves landed on her upper thigh. She screamed in pain as John strained on the rope. He coaxed the animal into the cubicle with a handful of fresh hay, while Rebecca, sitting in the muck, propped herself into a sitting position, leaning up against the wall.

"Can you walk on it?" asked John.

John helped the woman to an upright position, but she screamed when her shaking foot touched the ground. He grabbed her arm, draped it over his neck, and held her while she slowly hopped back to the farmhouse.

"I told you, John, but you just don't listen. I don't like that animal, and he doesn't like me," said Rebecca, her speech interrupted by smothered groans each time she took another step.

"Sorry," John mumbled.

Rebecca fell into a kitchen chair.

"You want I should look at it," asked John.

Rebecca's head shot up, her eyes shooting daggers.

"You've done enough damage, now please leave."

John scurried out of the house and Rebecca commenced her examination. A large and growing bruise on the upper thigh of her right leg looked worse than it felt. After some time, she hobbled about the house using an old broom as a makeshift cane.

Rebecca cursed her brother-in-law and the bull.

"I think it's time."

Fiona, experiencing contractions for most of the night, spoke to Mrs. Lobdell through teeth clenched in pain. Lobdell studied her patient, still six weeks from her due date. Dark circles appeared under the woman's eyes; she looked pale and weak, her nightgown and bed linens were sweat-soaked and bloodstained.

"It's too soon, Child. It's too soon. I'll send someone to fetch Doc McLean."

Fiona writhed in pain for another hour, before McLean finally arrived.

"Fiona, there is a midwife in the area. She is very good, her name is Betsy, and I believe she's had six children of her own."

"Just give me something for the pain, Doc, please."

McLean, secretly pleased, didn't like midwives, thinking doctors, even if they were male, more qualified to deal with an expectant mother. McLean carried a little chloroform in his bag. He poured it on a small hand towel provided by Mrs. Lobdell and held it over

Fiona's nose and mouth. The woman's eyes fluttered, and soon she was unconscious. McLean used his patient's silence to conduct an examination, this time with his hands and his eyes. Fiona, not far from giving birth, could not be given too much chloroform, as it would render the woman unable to assist with the birthing process. McLean breathed a sigh of relief when, less than an hour later, she woke with a scream. Mrs. Lobdell, on hand to assist with plenty of hot water and towels, held the woman's hand and wiped Fiona's sweaty brow.

"Almost there, Fiona," shouted McLean, positioned to catch the baby but leaving Fiona discreetly covered. A few contractions later, McLean made the announcement that Fiona waited for.

"You've given birth to a son."

Mrs. Lobdell, not given to emotional responses, smiled and cried simultaneously. She wrapped the tiny infant in a clean towel and presented him to the mother.

"He's beautiful."

Fiona, busy counting fingers and toes, kissed her newborn's forehead and whispered her reaction, "Thank you, Lord, thank you."

Her painful contractions resumed less than an hour later, Dr. McLean pressing on her abdomen as forcefully as he dared, to ensure expulsion of the afterbirth. The patient did not notice the look of fear on McLean's face when he realized that a portion of the placenta remained inside the mother's womb.

"Fiona, let's give the baby to Mrs. Lobdell. I want you to rest for a bit," said the doctor.

Mrs. Lobdell whisked the infant out of the room as McLean encouraged Fiona to breathe the remaining vapor in the used hand towel. Fiona's eyes fluttered and then closed. McLean went in search of Mrs. Lobdell.

"Is there a wet nurse in town?" he asked. "I don't like suck bottles, but we may need one."

Mrs. Lobdell knew of two possibilities, both black women, but questioned the doctor with her expression, even while nodding yes.

"I'm afraid she's in for some difficulty," he said, refusing to discuss the details but knowing full well that Fiona might soon contract the fever.

He returned to his sleeping patient, bracing himself for what was to come.

Chapter 19

A Visitor

Isaac wrote plenty of letters, but none to Rebecca.

He refused to write home, confused about his true feelings and still angry with her for giving him no choice but to leave. He wrote endless letters for other people, soldiers that were disabled, anxious, or, far too often, dying. Because there was little for soldiers to do, once the regiment had settled into its winter quarters, the corporal strongly suggested that Isaac put his formal education to good use. The enlistee, permitted to wander through the Post hospital, searched for victims who required assistance with reading, writing, or both.

On this Christmas morning, even though the camp cooks had prepared something special for dinner, Isaac made the daily trek to the Post hospital. Helping others seemed to reduce the pangs of his own loneliness, especially sharp during the holidays.

Isaac stopped at the foot of one cot, the wounded soldier immediately cocking his bandaged head, unable to see the person whose footsteps he heard.

"Is that you, Doc?" asked the wounded man.

"No, sir. It's Private Wells. I write letters for the men who can't."

Isaac studied his patient. Both of the man's legs were amputated above the knee, and his torso was wrapped in bandages, suggesting a gut wound. Only the man's nose and lips protruded from the mass of bandages which enclosed his entire head.

"Writing has become a challenge." said the soldier.

Isaac pulled his eyes off the two bandaged stumps to verify his patient's comment.

The wounded soldier, smiling through his blood-soaked rags, forced Isaac to laugh in relief.

"You haven't lost your sense of humor," said Isaac.

"No, but the rebs took my legs."

"Can I write a letter for you?"

"Sort of. I need to do a will."

Isaac stared at the bandages, uncertain as to how he should respond, if at all.

"I'm from Connecticut, I own a farm, no wife, no kids, but I got a few nieces and nephews."

Isaac looked away.

"No need to pretend, we both know I ain't gonna make it."

With some difficulty, the wounded man extended his right hand.

"William, but everyone calls me Willy."

Isaac reached for the outstretched hand.

"Isaac, Isaac Wells."

The two exchanged a few more pleasantries as Isaac reached into his haversack for a pen, paper, and ink.

Willy cocked his head.

"I can hear a ruckus down there, but you're gonna have to tell me what's going on."

Isaac turned toward the noise and could see several high-ranking officers escorting a short, stout, well-dressed woman. Behind them, walked a tall man holding a stovepipe hat. Isaac gasped.

"Oh, my Lord."

"What is it?" asked the blind man.

"You're not gonna believe it."

"What? What is it? Tell me, please."

"I believe you have visitors."

"Who is it?"

"The President and Mrs. Lincoln are here."

Isaac fixated on the first couple; the wounded man strained to hear more. Finally, the delegation arrived at Willy's bedside.

"Happy Christmas," said the First Lady. Willy's head turned up, his ear facing the woman's voice.

"Mrs. Lincoln, is that you?"

"Yes, and my dear husband is with me."

The tall man in black focused on the bedridden soldier. His frequent visits to the hospitals in DC made no difference. The sight of a dying man remained an emotional experience. Lincoln understood that the flat, unwrinkled blanket where there should have been legs and feet indicated a double amputee.

"God bless you, Boy."

Willy extended his hand, uncertain as to the exact direction of the presidential blessing, but accurately estimating the general direction of his president's voice.

"He already has, Mr. President, He already has," said Willy.

The soldier's bravery startled Lincoln. The President gripped the outstretched hand with both of his hands, his eyes blinking back tears, his lower lip curling in sorrow. He took a moment to compose himself but held onto the soldier's hand.

"I want you to get better," said Lincoln, as he grimaced and squeezed.

"Yes, Sir. I'll do my best."

The president nodded in Isaacs direction.

"How do you do."

I'm fine, Sir, thank you, Sir."

Lincoln moved to the next cot in line. Willy interrupted Isaac's trance.

"Come on Wells, we've got work to do."

"She's got the fever, Doc, and it's really bad."

Mrs. Lobdell looked as exhausted as she felt, tending to Fiona's infant boy and now tending to Fiona. McLean listened to the sick woman's heart and shook his head. He motioned to Mrs. Lobdell and shut the door behind them as they left the bedchamber.

"Cold compresses on her forehead and water when she asks for it. I've seen this before. There's nothing more I can do. It'll all be over in a couple of days."

Mrs. Lobdell clutched at her apron and dabbed at the tears in her eyes.

"The baby, what about the baby?"

McLean looked to the floor, closed his eyes, and shook his head.

I don't know, Mrs. Lobdell, I just don't know."

Mrs. Lobdell saw the doctor to the door and collapsed into the chair near Fiona's room. What an awful Christmas, she thought, Rebecca, still hobbling around even though the doc said no bones were broken, and now the old woman would be caring for an infant. Mrs. Lobdell cried into her apron, her grief interrupted by Fiona's loud moan.

"What is it, Child, what is it?" she asked, rushing to the dying lady's bedside. Fiona was conscious, her eyes red and swollen, her face flush from the fever. She struggled to get the words out, swallowing hard and hampered by dry swollen lips.

"Sip this," said Lobdell, reaching for a glass on the nightstand.

"My baby, my baby," Fiona whispered.

"He's doing fine, Fiona. Don't you worry about a thing. We don't even have a name for him yet. You'll have plenty of time with the baby, but first, you have to get better."

"Isaac."

"Excuse me," said Mrs. Lobdell.

"His name is Isaac," said the barely audible voice.

Mrs. Lobdell froze, the glass of water in her hand hovering over the bed. The sick woman's eyes fluttered shut; the room was deathly quiet.

"Isaac, after his father."

Mrs. Lobdell watched as Fiona's eyes fixed, her body now motionless.

Doctor Mclean pulled the sheet over Fiona's head.

"I'm sorry, Mrs. Lobdell, we did everything we could."

Mrs. Lobdell wiped her tears and nodded.

"There is one thing I failed to do. Perhaps you could help me," said Mclean.

The doctor gave Mrs. Lobdell a sealed letter.

"Would you mail this, please? I promised Fiona and then forgot."

Of course, Doctor, and thank you for all of your help.

"I will not have that bastard child in my home."

Rebecca and her mother rarely yelled at each other. Today, in the kitchen of the boarding house with the door shut, a different civil war, took place.

"Rebecca Lobdell, you are in my home now, and you will not use that language in my presence," said Mrs. Lobdell.

The daughter hissed at her mother.

"It's Rebecca Wells or did you forget?"

Mrs. Lobdell, pacing the floor and repeatedly wringing her hands, turned toward her daughter and spoke slowly.

"Rebecca, the baby has a father. Little Isaac is your husband's flesh and blood and the child needs a good home," she pleaded.

Rebecca slammed both of her open hands on the table, glared at her mother, and spat her response.

"No, I won't do it," she screamed. "And you can't make me."

Mrs. Lobdell turned away, her arms folded, and her head down. Rebecca shouted even louder.

"I am not that baby's mother. My husband fathered that child with a prostitute. Must the whole world be witness to his reckless behavior? Am I to be humiliated? Is that what you want, Momma?"

Mrs. Lobdell, her face now twisted in agony, muffled her sobs with the apron she always wore. Rebecca, sensing she had prevailed, muttered a mechanical goodbye and left.

John was waiting for Rebecca in front of the boarding house, feeding the old mare a handful of hay and checking the hitch and leathers which tethered his horse to the aging buckboard.

"Took you long enough," said John.

He did not want Rebecca tagging along on his weekly journey into town and remained particularly irked that an inspection of the newly-opened tavern he once owned would no longer occur. He clucked his tongue; and the backboard groaned forward.

"We must travel to Albany, the sooner, the better,"

"We?" John asked.

"Yes, there is an orphanage there."

John smiled, impressed with Rebecca's strategy, but sensing an opportunity.

"You don't need me. You take a steamer to Whitehall and then a train to Albany. Your husband did it, twice."

"A woman all alone, with a baby, and on her way to an orphanage. How do you think that would look?"

"What's in it for me?" he asked.

"I will pay for all of our expenses."

That's not enough."

"What do you want from me?"

"Rebecca, your husband is gone; he may be dead for all we know. And now, you're cleaning up his mess. Have you even heard from him yet?"

"No," Rebecca said, her eyes welling up with tears.

"I'll go with you to Albany, Rebecca, because I care for you and because I want to do the right thing by you. But you have to give me a chance. Can we at least be friends?"

John pulled on the reins and brought the wagon to a halt. They were in the middle of the road to Port Kent surrounded by fields and trees. He swung his right hand over her shoulder and pulled the woman close. Rebecca did not resist.

"It will all work out. Trust me," he said.

Chapter 20

Washington and Albany

Isaac Wells, enjoying a rare day of no orders, lay in his cot, pretending to sleep.

"On your feet, Private."

The sergeant, ordinarily a pleasant man, did not smile.

"Get dressed and look sharp. You'll be driving Congressman Kellogg and his aide around the city."

Isaac's eyebrows shot up.

"Orlando Kellogg, from Essex County?"

"Yup."

The sergeant explained that Kellogg, in Washington on business, stopped to visit the 118th, because the regiment had been recruited entirely within his district. The colonel offered the Congressman a carriage and a driver for Kellogg's remaining visits, a necessity in the spring, as the streets of the Capitol were awash in mud and filth.

"Report to the colonel's office in thirty minutes," said the officer.

Isaac wasted no time and in a short while, shook hands with the distinguished-looking representative from Essex County.

"Our first stop is the Willard Hotel. Do you know where it is?"

"Yes, sir."

"Let's go."

Isaac drove the two men to their destination and waited not more than a half-hour when they returned with a third gentleman in their midst. They continued a discussion that started in the building.

"What is it you want me to do? What can I do?" asked the third man.

"Mr. Assistant Secretary, I want you to countermand your order for the removal of the customs house in Plattsburgh."

Isaac, from his perch in the front of the horse-drawn barouche, learned that the port of entry, once in Plattsburgh, suddenly and without warning, moved to Rouses Point. Kellogg wanted the order reversed and would not take no for an answer. The next stop was the office of the Treasury Secretary, Salmon Chase. Isaac, forced to wait again, watched as Kellogg emerged from the building with just his aide. They were both smiling,

"Do you think there is a precedent case which he can use to justify your request?" asked the aide.

"I have no case in mind, but the books must be full of them," said the Congressman. "I'm sure the secretary will do as we wish."

"And now I'd like to call on an old friend," said Kellogg.

"Who might that be?" asked Isaac.

The aid was grinning.

"President Lincoln."

Isaac sat a little straighter as he pulled the carriage to a stop just yards from the front entrance of the Executive Mansion. As the congressman and his assistant stepped off the carriage, Kellogg stopped and turned toward Isaac."

"Don't you want to meet Mr. Lincoln?"

Isaac scrambled off the carriage and followed the Congressman into the White House. Several people waited to see the President, but Kellogg insisted that his card be brought to Lincoln's attention. In minutes, the usher called for Kellogg. Lincoln was sitting with his back to the door when the trio entered his office. One leg was propped up on the office table; his white shin fully exposed. He stretched his right arm over his left shoulder and after grasping Kellogg's hand rose to his feet.

"My dear friend, I'm glad to see you, take a chair."

When Kellogg introduced Isaac to the president, Lincoln spoke to Kellogg instead.

"I'm glad to see that you know the kind of company to keep. I hardly feel respectable these days, if I don't have a soldier for a companion. Citizen's dress doesn't amount to much these days. Is this one of your constituents?"

"Yes," replied Kellogg, "His regiment was wholly raised in my district. They are all my boys."

The presidential audience lasted for a half-hour, both men serving in the same session of Congress, and wanting to relive the good old days. The two reminisced and laughed heartily, as the usher continued to place cards in front of the President. Kellogg took note and rose to leave.

"Don't hurry," said Lincoln, as he picked up a handful of cards.

"These gentlemen will wait. They all want something. You want nothing, and I have enjoyed your call," Lincoln said.

But Kellogg insisted. The president said his goodbyes and then turned to Isaac to shake his hand.

"I count you and every soldier as a friend."

"Thank you, Sir."

Isaac left the White House almost forgetting all that he left behind in Keeseville, New York. For this great man, he would sacrifice everything, unto life itself.

Mrs. Lobdell looked at her daughter through swollen, bloodshot eyes, blowing her nose and wiping away the tears.

Rebecca did her best to ignore the woman, focusing on the baby, the blankets and wraps necessary for the long trip to Albany, and the cloth bag which contained the infant's meager belongings.

"It's best this way, Momma. Please understand."

Mrs. Lobdell shook her head in disagreement. She stepped toward the girl and then stopped short.

"You are not the daughter that I once knew."

Rebecca picked up the baby and its belongings and left.

John Wells couldn't care less about Isaac's love child. But he looked forward to the trip. Hours alone with Rebecca to work his charms plus an overnight stay in Albany presented many possibilities, he thought. When the threesome boarded their steamer to Whitehall, they looked like a family, the baby, resembling his uncle, John. But John saw the trip as an opportunity to act on the lust for Rebecca that slithered and twitched in his unconscious mind. John, bored on the farm, could no longer afford his long-standing habit of booze and whores but his sister-in-law was now available and vulnerable.

"My word, it's freezing in here," said Rebecca, as she positioned herself in the stateroom close to the tiny wood-stove."

"Well, it is April. I'm surprised the boat is even running this time of the year. The lake is usually frozen over," said John.

He squeezed onto the bench, forcing Rebecca up against the wall. He swung his arm around her shoulder and pulled Rebecca toward him.

"Stay close, I'll keep you warm," he said, pulling her even closer.

Rebecca focused on the baby, now crying loudly from the cold.

"Noisy little brat, isn't he?" said John.

Unable to tolerate the noise any longer, John left for the upper deck.

An elderly lady, sitting opposite Rebecca, waited until John disappeared.

"Take the baby to the boiler room. It's nice and warm down there."

Rebecca inquired of the ship's attendant and was directed down a short set of steps.

"You not suposta be here, Missus. But I see you gots a babychild."

Rebecca stopped and studied the man, easily the biggest she had ever seen, black and covered with coal dust and sweat. The baby's screams drowned her fears.

"Please?" she asked.

"I is gonna shut the doh so as no one gonna see you. Is dat ok?"

Rebecca thought for a moment and then nodded. He flipped over an empty vegetable crate and propped it up against the cabin wall.

"Yous kin sit here iffin you want."

Rebecca took the man's offer and smiled her thanks, as little Isaac stopped crying, working feverishly on his suck bottle.

"My name is Rebecca," she said.

"Elijah. Most folks call me Eli."

Rebecca's free arm jerked, but she decided against shaking the man's hand. Eli shoveled another scoop of coal into the fiery furnace. Rebecca thought her hesitancy went unnoticed.

"S'alright. I gits dirty down here. Can't hep it."

He threw another shovel of coal into the blazing inferno, not quite as full as the first one.

"My momma had a yung un, she just love that thing to death."

"Boy or girl," asked Rebecca, her courage blossoming in the heat.

"A boy. She name em Moses cuz Moses in da good book."

"Where are your mama and little brother now?" she asked.

Eli stopped shoveling and stared into the fire.

"The boss man dun sold Moses."

Rebecca's eyes grew wide.

"You were slaves. Your mama, is she?"

Rebecca's voice trailed off.

Eli, now shoveling at a furious pace, didn't stop until he struggled to breathe. The sweat ran off his brow.

"Broke her heart," he said, panting and leaning on the shovel for support.

"The boss man dun horsewhip the house niggah, he was dat mad."

"What happened?" Rebecca asked.

"She dun hung herself."

Eli leaned against the far wall and stared at the fire.

"Ain't no woman alive can lose their baby and still wanna live."

Rebeca, her eyes shut tight in an effort to staunch the flow of tears, cradled the sleeping baby, holding him just a little closer.

Rebecca's conversation with Elisha tormented the virgin bride for the remainder of her trip.

How could anyone rip a child from its mother and then sell it like a piglet? And yet, the sleeping child she carried would soon be alone, Mother Nature tearing him from Fiona's arms, in a manner no less cold and cruel than the slave owner that sold Moses. Rebecca, unable to squash the fleeting thought that she wasn't much better than the plantation owner, wondered how she could care for a helpless child, operate a farm, and do it all, without a husband.

Her brother-in-law had no such compunctions, thought Rebecca. He treated the baby, his nephew, as nothing more than a noisy nuisance. But he did accompany her on the trip to Albany, and for that she should be grateful. The stream of confused thoughts erased the memory of her train ride from Whitehall into Albany. The Wells family, in name only, pulled into the station after dark. A short, buggy ride placed the trio in the lobby of the Delavan House, in search of a room.

"Please sign the register, sir," said the desk clerk, pushing the oversized book toward John and turning it right side up as he did so.

"That'll be one dollar, in advance."

Rebecca held the infant in one arm as she searched her bag for a few coins.

"Your room has a beautiful view of the Capitol building, Mr. and Mrs. Wells. Enjoy your stay."

John grinned at the desk clerk, Rebecca frowned.

"I am not Mrs. Wells. Well actually, I am Mrs. Wells, but this man is not my husband. And the baby is. Never mind."

Rebecca grew angrier as John's grin turned to laughter.

"I want my own room," she yelled, slamming two more coins on the front desk. The clerk, his eyes wide with curiosity, slowly pushed the register in Rebecca's direction, alternating his gaze from Rebecca, to John, to the baby and then back to Rebecca.

"Do you need help with your bags?" asked the clerk.

"No," she responded, carrying her purse, the baby, and the bag, as she stormed up the stairwell.

John followed behind, keeping a respectful distance.

Chapter 21

Under Fire

Isaac slipped into the back of the tent used for church services, not surprised that so many soldiers had come to pray.

The 118th received its marching orders and would soon board the transport *Utica* for a trip down the Potomac. Their announced destination, Fort Monroe, but everyone guessed that Suffolk was their final objective. The small town in Virginia, under siege by Confederate General Longstreet, required assistance. The 118th would reinforce Union defenses, under the command of General Peck.

The steamboat went no further than Norfolk, where the regiment boarded platform cars to get to their final destination. At a stop for water, in the middle of Dismal Swamp, the boom of artillery could be heard. Isaac's blonde-haired, battle buddy, Thad Stevens, questioned one guard at the water station.

"Is that artillery? Are we getting close?"

The sentry let his head droop and closed his eyes.

"Veal for the meat grinder."

"What does that mean?" asked Thad.

"You'll find out soon enough," said the guard.

As the train pulled away, Thad questioned Isaac.

What in tarnation was he talking about?"

"Fresh meat, Thad. He was saying that we are fresh meat and the rebs are going to grind us up."

Thad opened his mouth to object but was drowned out by the

sound of cannon fire, now louder than the train's engine. The regiment arrived at the Suffolk train station late that evening. The big guns were silent now, cold, steady rain falling while the men pitched their tents as fast as they could. In the morning, they were joined by several other regiments and ordered to build a series of earthen works along the riverbanks. The 118th was given the lead and told to avoid open spaces as much as possible. Rebel sharpshooters were as ubiquitous as the pine trees in which they hid.

Isaac and his buddy, side-by-side, followed the bank of the Nansemond River to their destination.

"I'm wishing I was back in Keeseville right about now," said Isaac, as he picked a grayback out of his scalp. The lice had appeared at the Suffolk train station, and the raw recruit thought he could win his battle with the pests.

"And we enlisted," said Thad, laughing at the irony.

A shot rang out, and a branch just inches from Isaac's head was split in two. Isaac fell to the ground and searched in every direction.

"Where is that reb bastard?"

Thad was crouching behind a large tree, occasionally poking his head out.

"I can't see a thing, but it sounded like it came from across the river."

The Nansemond River narrowed enough at certain points in its path that such a shot could be made. Isaac scrambled to the safety of the deep woods and yelled at Thad to do the same.

"I'm right behind you."

Another shot rang out and Isaac turned. Thad was standing alongside a tree, his eyes fixed on the bloody stump that used to be his left hand.

"I've been shot."

Isaac screamed.

"Get down you fool."

The rebel sharpshooter fired once more. Thad's head exploded. Isaac, shut his eyes, as a shower of blood, bone, and gray matter pelted his face and uniform. For a brief moment, he remained motionless, transfixed by the sound and sight of his friend's headless body as it slammed into the muddy ground. Another shot sent Isaac running even deeper into the woods. He ran as fast as he could and refused to stop. The trees, bushes and his fellow soldiers were nothing more than a blur. He would not stop.

"Hey, you're going the wrong way, Soldier."

The large man in blue put his foot out, and Isaac fell headfirst into a patch of saplings, breaking several with his fall. As he lay there on his stomach, gasping for air, his head swiveling in a desperate search for the rifle he dropped, Isaac felt two large hands pulling on the back of his collar.

"The war's that way," said the voice, as he spun Isaac around.

Isaac recognized his sergeant and closed his eyes, intent on getting the words out.

"They shot Thad, Sarge; they shot Thad–he's dead."

Isaac wanted the sergeant to correct him; it was all just a bad dream, Thad was still alive, but the sergeant didn't cooperate.

"Ain't nothing you can do for your friend. His time was up, and now he's gone. You wanna help? Go get those rebel bastards that shot him. Move it. Now!"

The sarge pushed Isaac's rifle into the boy's chest and pulled a dirty, blood-stained cap over the boy's head. Isaac paused as if to confirm the big man's orders. The veteran placed his nose within an inch of Isaac's face.

"Go."

Isaac did not stop running, until he was surrounded by blue uniforms.

John waited until he could no longer hear the baby crying.

He tiptoed down the hallway and put his ear up against the door to Rebecca's room, several times. He slowly turned the porcelain knob, but Rebecca had locked the door. He grimaced, thought for a moment, and then knocked several times, but not too hard. After a while, he could hear the key turning in the door and wondered to himself why Rebecca did not first inquire as to her visitor's identity.

"I heard you the first two times you came to my door," she said.

Rebecca glared at John over an imaginary set of spectacles, a hand perched on each hip, and with a thin smirk on her lips. John blushed but quickly recovered.

"I'm just checking on you and the baby."

He looked over her shoulder as if to prove his sincerity.

"The baby's fine. What do you want?"

"Well, I was downstairs having a few drinks, and I thought maybe you would like to join me."

"John. I can't leave the baby alone, and in case you have forgotten, I am a married woman."

John scowled his disappointment

"Rebecca, I thought we were friends. That's why I agreed to this trip in the first place."

"I'm paying for all of our expenses plus the extra hired hand you insisted we needed. What more do you want?"

Rebecca didn't wait for a response and reached for the open door.

"I'll show you what I want," he said.

He grabbed Rebecca by the shoulders, pulled her close, and pressed his lips against her half-open mouth. When John released the woman, she tried to slap the man, but then he pushed Rebecca hard enough to send her sprawling backward onto the bed. John kicked the door shut, and immediately, the baby started to cry. Rebecca's eyes rolled to the back of her head. She grew faint but still resisted. He bit her lips and shoved his face into her chest. The smell of booze surrounded Rebecca's face. He straddled the woman and tugged at the hem of her nightdress. The demons are back, Rebecca thought. She heard the baby screaming and for a brief moment, opened her eyes. She couldn't budge her assailant, the walls spun, her eyes fluttered shut. Rebecca stopped moving. John paused his attack to throw a pillow at the screaming child in the cradle on the floor. The infant's bed rocked violently, and the child yelled even louder. John searched the room for the kid's suck bottle, found it on the nightstand and shoved it into the baby's mouth. John's strategy worked until little Isaac discovered that his bottle no longer contained any milk.

"Shut up you little bastard."

John buried the baby in blankets and used Rebecca's wrap for good measure. The screams were muffled, and John had time to focus on his victim. A portion of her bosom was exposed because he had ripped her nightdress. He sat on the side of her bed and caressed the smooth skin on her face and chest. Breathing heavy now, he could feel the stirring in his loins.

The baby's flailing arms succeeded in removing a portion of the makeshift gag and the screams grew loud once again. John winced, the noise was distracting him.

"That's it, Kid, you're sleeping in my room tonight."

He wrapped the child in a blanket and covered the kid's face and head with another blanket, muffling the baby's cries once more. A quick glance confirmed that Rebecca was still unconscious. As he turned toward the door, several loud knocks stopped him in his tracks.

"Is everything all right, Mrs. Wells? May I help you in any way?"

John recognized the desk clerk's voice and squeezed his eyes tight, trying to concentrate. He unwrapped his young victim, returned the baby to its crib, and opened the door. The desk clerk greeted him, with several hotel guests now in the hallway and observing the scene.

"I'm terribly sorry, Mr. Wells, but we've had some complaints."

One lady, a few doors down, approached the two men.

"Perhaps I can help," she said.

The offer of assistance came from an older woman, still in her nightdress but wrapped in a shawl. Once again, John's mind raced.

"Mrs. Wells is feeling rather poorly, and I think the baby is sick, too," he said.

The old woman squeezed past the desk clerk and brushed John to one side.

"I'll need some fresh milk, hot water, and towels."

"Yes, ma'am." said the grateful clerk, as he rushed down the hallway. John stared the spectators back into their rooms.

"How did she rip her night dress?" asked the woman.

"Well, she fainted and I grabbed her to break the fall and. . ."

"Never mind. Go and see what's taking that man so long with the milk."

John scurried down the stairs, through the lobby, and then out the door.

He did not search for the desk clerk.

Isaac, now convinced that everyone in the regiment was staring at him, wanted to run and hide.

Yaller dog. That's what they called cowards. Isaac was a yaller dog, he thought.

"I need five volunteers," said the lieutenant.

"We've got the rebs on the run except for one place on the line. I aim to bust them up. Who's with me?"

Isaac's hand shot up. Now it became obvious, the lieutenant and everyone else stared at the boy. He didn't care. When soaking wet, covered with mud, and exhausted, the line between courage in the face of death and a reckless disregard for your own life is no longer obvious. Add anger to that formula and the warrior in question becomes a killing machine. Isaac, angry that his life had come to this, an endless fight with an unseen enemy to free slaves that he neither used nor owned, focused on his destiny–several more years of rotten food, lice, and loneliness. Rebecca, law school, and the family farm now nothing more than pleasant memories. A bullet in the head is quick and painless, he thought–an end to his endless misery.

"I'm in," Isaac said.

The lieutenant got five soldiers to volunteer. The men gathered around their commanding officer.

"The rebs have a small breastwork made of planks, and they're hold up behind it. We're gonna flank 'em and take them by surprise. Fix bayonets."

Isaac did as he was told, surprised by his calm demeanor in the face of almost certain death. He fixated on his coat and one blood stain, in particular, that took the shape of a woman's head. It reminded him of Rebecca's red hair.

"I'm ready," he said.

A small chorus of "me-toos" prompted the lieutenant.

"Follow me."

The six men walked quietly through a small patch of trees and underbrush, flanking the breastworks on the east side to keep the sun at their backs. The lieutenant waived his hand, and the men separated themselves into a straight line with about ten feet between each. Now less than fifty yards from the enemy's lair, Isaac stood nearest to the lieutenant. The officer pointed his rifle to the sky and froze. When he had everyone's attention, he dropped the weapon to eye level, aimed it forward, and screamed. All the man yelled. Isaac easily outran his comrades. He fired his Enfield, and one of the enemy soldiers went down. Two gray uniforms reached for their side arms. Isaac, now at close range, could hear the Minié balls whiz by his head. He plunged his bayonet into the first soldier and used the butt of his rifle to dispatch the other rebel. A third soldier, not yet old enough to grow whiskers, froze in place, mesmerized by the blood-covered maniac in his midst. Isaac pulled his sidearm from its holster and leveled it not two feet from the soldier's face. The warrior in gray opened his mouth to object, but Isaac used it as a target, sending most of the boy's brains onto a nearby soldier. The crazed man in blue was ready to fire again when he noticed that the remaining rebels, a half dozen of them, dropped their weapons and now stood with their arms and hands pointed skyward. Isaac paused long enough for the lieutenant and the remainder of the contingent to arrive on the scene. Still catching his breath, Isaac felt the lieutenant's congratulatory slap on his back.

"You gonna fight this war all by yourself?"

The lieutenant and his men grinned their approval and admiration for Isaac's reckless behavior. Isaac continued to point his revolver at the soldiers in gray.

"Which one of you bastards killed my friend?"

None were sharpshooters, but it didn't seem to matter to Isaac.

"Easy, Boy, easy. They're prisoners of war now," said the lieutenant.

For a moment, Isaac refused to budge.

"If they were my prisoners, I'd kill every last one of 'em."

Isaac holstered his weapon, spat on the ground in front of him, and stormed off.

Chapter 22

The Orphanage

"Can you hear me, Mrs. Wells?"

Rebecca's eyes fluttered open, focusing with great difficulty on the woman's voice and the man with the mustache. She recognized him as the desk clerk at the hotel, but not the woman. Rebecca's eyes opened wide, and she struggled to sit up.

"The baby, where is the baby?"

"He's sleeping in my room, next-door, been changed and fed and he's happier than a lark. No need for you to worry," said the lady.

"What happened?" Rebecca asked, but then she remembered what happened, John pushing her onto the bed, a loud bang, the awful smell of booze and sweat. And the demons.

"We can't seem to find your husband," said the woman.

"He's not my husband."

"Well, he's disappeared, whoever he is."

Rebecca asked for some water and then acknowledged her benefactors.

"Thank you. Thank you both. You have been most kind."

The desk clerk smiled, and the lady with the shawl introduced herself.

"Everyone calls me Bella. Are you feeling a little better?"

"Yes. Can I see my baby now?"

"Yes, of course."

As Bella left to retrieve baby Isaac, Rebecca corrected her mental error. He's not my baby, she thought. That Fiona woman is the real mother. Bella placed the child in Rebecca's outstretched arms. The young girl examined the child and kissed the boy on his forehead. Relieved, she looked up and smiled.

"Thank you, Bella. Now if you don't mind, I think we'll get some rest."

Her new friends left the room, and Rebecca fell asleep with the baby at her side. He stirred once but was otherwise content with his temporary caretaker.

"I need a carriage. Can you arrange that for me?"

Rebecca, with baby Isaac in tow, did not disclose her destination to the head waiter. She finished her coffee while repeatedly telling herself it was the right thing to do. Baby Isaac would most likely be adopted by a loving couple and grow up in a nice house. I would be a poor mother, she thought. I'm already a poor wife.

The carriage ride to the orphanage went quickly, and the baby had made no sort of fuss. He was a good baby. Rebecca made a mental note to tell the orphanage staff they were fortunate to receive such a well-behaved infant. She paid the driver twice what he was owed and instructed him not to leave.

"This won't take long," she said.

Rebecca thought she saw a look of disgust on the driver's face but wasn't sure.

"Was Mr. Clemmons, the Director, expecting you?"

The woman in the orphanage that confronted Rebecca did not hide her irritation.

"No, I do not have an appointment, but I do have a baby, and he needs a good home."

The older woman looked down on the girl because she was taller than Rebecca but Rebecca sensed a distinct air of condescension.

"I'm not the mother."

"Of course, you're not."

The matron, dressed entirely in white, smiled exposing none of her teeth and walked away, shouting over her shoulder.

"Wait here, please."

Rebecca scanned the lobby and spied a wooden bench on which to rest. She had made herself comfortable, the baby still in her arms, when a young boy, no more than six, came running into the lobby. The crying and screaming boy looked behind him as if being chased. The child scampered onto the bench and grabbed Rebecca's free arm. He hugged her tight.

"Help me. Please help me," he said.

Before Rebecca could respond, another matron, also in white, appeared in the lobby brandishing a walking stick. She spotted her prey on the bench.

"William, come here this instant."

The boy, trembling violently and shaking his head no, refused to budge, squirming even closer to Rebecca. The matron did not repeat her request. She jerked the boy from the bench and beat the child on his buttocks and back, as she dragged him down the hallway. Rebecca winced with each blow of the stick and couldn't breathe easy, until the slam of a distant door silenced the boy's cries.

"Mr. Clemmons will see you now."

Rebecca, still reeling from the matron's display of discipline, followed the white dress into an office, nicely furnished with stain glass windows, an oversized desk and several overstuffed chairs. Behind the desk, set a small, bespectacled man who, although bald, sported a shaped, handlebar mustache. He said nothing as Rebecca stood there, with infant in hand, waiting to be noticed. Minutes passed before the man paused and looked up from his newspaper. He was unsmiling and annoyed with the interruption.

"May I help you?"

"Yes, I have come here about the baby. His name is."

"Does the child belong to you?"

"Well, yes and no, you see my husband enlisted, but before we–got married."

"For goodness sake's woman, is the child yours or not?"

"No."

"Where is the mother?"

"She's dead."

"Where is the father?"

Rebecca hesitated.

"I don't know."

"Well, it doesn't matter. The answer is no."

"I'm sorry, I don't understand."

"We have the rooms and staff for no more than six infants. We are currently housing ten of them. You and your baby will have to go elsewhere."

"He's not my baby."

"So you said."

"Is there another orphanage in Albany?"

"There are two, one in Albany and another in Troy. But don't bother. There's a war on if you haven't heard and both institutions are full."

Rebecca looked at the bundle in her arms, a confusing stream of thoughts swarming in her mind. The Director removed his spectacles with both hands, held them aloft, and dropped them on the desk with a loud clatter.

"Is there anything else, Mrs . . ?"

Rebecca's eyes flashed as she stepped closer to the man's desk. The little girl, now a woman, summoned the courage to fight back. This bully, she thought, like the long line of bullies that came before him, needed to be stopped. Rebecca, too tired and too angry to accept his abuse, leaned over the man's desk as if addressing a recalcitrant two-year-old.

"It's Wells. Mrs. Isaac Wells. And yes, there is one more thing. While I was waiting to see you, one of your matrons used a stick to beat a scared, little boy, and for no apparent reason. I wish I had a stick, Mr. Clemmons, because if I did, I would give you a thrashing that you would not soon forget."

Mr. Clemmons sputtered and retrieved his spectacles.

"Now see here, Mrs. Wells."

"Good day, Mr. Clemmons."

The day-long journey back to Plattsburgh gave John plenty of time to consider his options.

He could not return to the family farm, Rebecca would show up sooner or later. Given his vicious behavior at the hotel in Albany, she was likely to contact Sheriff Bromley. John's history with the sheriff made incarceration a distinct possibility. As he disembarked the steamboat, John's desperation grew. He had no place to go, no friends on which he could rely, and just a few coins in his pocket. He walked to the nearest tavern, Plattsburgh had lots of them and threw one of his coins on the bar. While sipping his beer, John studied the barmaid, middle-aged, plain, and with plenty of wrinkles, but when she made eye contact, he put his head down and walked to the door. He lost interest.

A broadside, nailed to the inside of the door, caught his attention. Clinton County offered a seventy-five dollar bounty for any man willing to enlist in the US Army. The nine-month enlistment period included an additional one hundred dollars if the term of enlistment was successfully completed. Essex County offered no bounty, as they achieved their mandated quota with volunteers. Volunteers like Isaac, thought John, who enlisted for three years and received thirteen dollars a month for risking their lives. *What an idiot,* he thought. Clinton County paid a bounty for less effort and who says you must serve the entire nine months? John made a beeline to the barracks on the other end of the village, in search of Timmons, the recruiting sergeant whose name was on the broadside.

"When do I get the seventy-five bucks?"

The man in blue, himself a volunteer, frowned as he explained to John that the Oath of Enlistment must first be administered. In less than a week, the newly formed NY 16th Calvary Regiment would travel to Albany where uniforms, equipment, and horses would be issued.

"Can you ride?" asked the sargeant.

"Since I was old enough to walk, is that good enough?"

"Go see the doc."

The sergeant pointed, and John submitted to the physical exam, nothing more than a cursory look and a few questions. Later, John experienced difficulty with the oath, struggling to remain serious when they got to that part that said, *'I take this obligation freely, without any mental reservation or purpose of evasion and that I will well and faithfully discharge the duties of the office on which I am about to enter, so help me God.'* After receiving his bounty, John grinned his appreciation, but the enlistee's ulterior motive remained. He had no intention of serving in the Army. The only question was when and how he would elude his superiors.

After a few days of drilling, a monotonous past time if ever there was one, thought John, the recruits organized for their march to the docks in Plattsburgh. A steamer to Whitehall and then a series of trains would deliver the new regiment to its first assignment, the defense of Washington.

John correctly surmised that the dockside scene would be chaotic and crowded. When the sergeant started his company roll call, John announced to his chums that he had to "take a leak." He ducked behind a nearby building and didn't wait for the sergeant to reach 'W'. With no uniform to distinguish him from other passersby, John made his way south and eventually to Keeseville. With plenty of money in his pocket and no person in Keeseville knowledgeable of his deception, John settled in at the Ausable House. He had to plan his next move.

But first, a beer.

Chapter 23

Rejected

Isaac's bravery on the field of battle earned him several amenities.

Although grateful for the extra rations and the exemption from "sink" duty, (digging latrines), Isaac spent most of his downtime alone in his dog tent. The boy's anger and bitterness grew by the day. He ignored the open-air church services and, in a stunning departure from his life-long Christian ways, played cards. The paymaster, now missing for six weeks, forced the men to play for bragging rights and the occasional trinket. Isaac won a pipe with some tobacco. He never smoked but lit up anyway, desperate to leave behind his wholesome, innocent, and depressing past.

As he lay in his tent, brooding about the lack of mail from home, he wondered about the woman he had married. Rebecca, his wife but in name only, stood in sharp contrast to the women of the war. There were Negro servants attached to several officers, often engaged in activities far removed from cleaning and cooking meals. Isaac envied those officers when they bragged about the "horizontal refreshments" provided by their servants. Isaac, except for a one-night stand with a hooker, would still be a virgin. He lusted for a woman, Negro or otherwise.

Isaac slept for most of the day, for the next couple of days, in part, because the weather improved, he was neither cold nor wet, but mostly because he was bored. When the entire regiment moved further down the railroad tracks, the young soldier was grateful for something to do. A few troops discovered an active farm near the new campsite and investigated. Isaac, accompanied by his sergeant and four colleagues, introduced themselves to a farmer and his wife. The couple and their two, grown daughters spun cotton and smoked pipes, causing knowing looks among the men. The women offered several dozen pairs of socks to the men, who leaned on their sergeant for a temporary loan.

One of the pipe smoking daughters took a liking to Isaac, and the two wandered into a field taking advantage of the shade, under a large pine tree. The young lady, Isaac guessed her age as being twenty or so, continued puffing on her pipe.

"Where are you from, Private?"

"Keeseville, New York."

"Never heard of the place."

Isaac was mentally comparing the girl to Rebecca and Fiona. She wore short black, uncombed hair, a torn and dirty dress, a deep tan, and a man's demeanor. The sharp contrast with Isaac's limited experience puzzled the boy, but the pipe-smoking farm girl guessed his thoughts.

"You got a girl back home?" she asked.

Isaac looked off into the distance.

"No, I don't."

"Do you like fishin'?"

"Yes."

"Follow me."

She grabbed the young soldier by the hand and walked him a few hundred yards to a nearby stream.

"This is my favorite fishin' spot."

"What do you catch?" he asked.

She grinned and shook her head.

"Catfish, Stupid. Ain't you got 'em up north?"

She sat on the bank, reached for her pipe, and took a few deep drags. The pipe refused to cooperate. Isaac chose not to answer her question and sat down beside her.

"I had a reb soldier down here a few months ago. Handsome fella, just like you."

She leaned in and kissed Isaac on the cheek. Isaac looked around and kissed her lips.

"What are you doing, Soldier?"

"I thought. Well, you said."

"I didn't say anything, Boy."

She rose to her knees with her breasts just inches from his face. Isaac was confused but leaned forward. She pushed him on his back and straddled his legs.

"When's the last time you got paid, Private?"

We haven't been paid in six weeks."

"You got any money at all?"

"No, ma'am."

"At least the reb had a few Confederate dollars."

She rose, slapped the open end of her pipe on the palm of her hand, and climbed up the riverbank.

"You comin'?"

Isaac nodded.

Rebecca, still angry but no longer frightened, planned her future as she rode to the Albany train station.

Just a few weeks ago, the very thought of Fiona in bed with her husband, sent Rebecca into a furious rage. Today, more concerned that no harm came to the child, she pushed the angry thought from her head and focused on a renewed determination to meet her responsibilities as a surrogate mother and farm owner.

As she boarded the train, her thoughts shifted to the man who caused her bodily harm, John Wells. She did not expect to find him in the Keeseville home but wondered what he would do and where he would go. By the time she boarded the steamboat to

Plattsburgh, she had resolved to report the incident to Sheriff Bromley. And while she had no ownership interest in the homestead, Rebecca intended to occupy the farmhouse and run the farm with hired hands as best she could. Her marriage to Isaac Wells gave her that right.

When the stage arrived in Keeseville, she directed the driver to her mother's boarding house. Mrs. Lobdell greeted her daughter and the infant child with tears in her eyes and a big hug.

"I'm going to need your help, Momma," said Rebecca.

Mrs. Lobdell kissed her daughter and ushered them into the kitchen. Rebecca recounted the events in Albany, making particular mention of her brother-in-law.

"I know it's a non-Christian thing to say, Momma, but John Wells is an evil man."

"I'm worried about you be'in back on the farm and all alone out there. What if he returns?"

"I'm going to the sheriff's office from here. I'll be fine."

The two women spent the rest of the afternoon fussing over the baby, Isaac.

For the first time in a long time, Rebecca smiled constantly.

When Rebecca left the sheriff's office, she nearly collided with two soldiers.

The blue uniforms excused themselves, intent on a visit with the sheriff. She walked to her waiting carriage and placed the baby on a large pile of blankets and wraps. As she searched her bag for his suck bottle, a familiar voice called.

"Mrs. Wells, congratulations on the new baby."

Edgar Putnam smiled broadly.

"May I see him? It is a boy, is it not?"

Without waiting for Rebecca to respond, the schoolmaster peered into the carriage.

"He looks just like his father."

Rebecca grimaced, thought better of it, and then smiled."

"Have you heard from our warrior friend?" he asked.

"No, Mr. Putnam. I have sent several letters. I don't know where he is but I pray that he is alive and well."

"Excuse me, Mrs. Wells?"

One of the soldiers interrupted Rebecca and Mr. Putnam. Putnam offered to leave but Rebecca reached for the schoolmaster's arm.

"Please stay."

She addressed the soldier.

"May I help you?"

"We understand that you filed a complaint against your brother-in-law. We want you to know that we're looking for him, too."

Rebecca glanced at Mr. Putnam and closed her eyes. The soldier continued, "He enlisted, ma'am, took the oath, collected the bounty, and then went AWOL."

"I haven't seen him," she said.

"If he shows up, please contact the sheriff. He'll send a telegraph."

"Yes, sir, I will."

"Thank you, ma'am."

The soldier tipped his hat, smiled toward Putnam, and crossed the street.

"May I be of any assistance, Mrs. Wells?" said Putnam.

"No. Thank you, Mr. Putnam. I must be on my way."

John Wells paced the floor of his room, smoothed his ruffled hair, and repeatedly gazed out the window of his tiny room at the Ausable House.

Holed up at the Ausable House for almost a week now, John drank himself to sleep almost every evening. The tiny room, with one small window to the back alley, grew smaller by the day. Once,

John counted the flowers on the wall-papered surfaces of his bedchamber. Tonight, instead of taking his meal in the room, John ventured out. A moonless night reduced the chances he might encounter anyone, much less someone he knew, or so he thought.

The soldier for a day took a leisurely stroll down the main street in Keeseville. He ducked his head into the recently opened Sample's Tavern, but only for a moment. It looked nice, he thought, and John fumed that he no longer owned the place. He considered a visit with Sheriff Bromley, to see if any progress had been made with Jed Sample. The bastard still owed him several hundred dollars. He dismissed the idea, recalling his status as a soldier on the run. His slow walk back to the Ausable House triggered an epiphany of sorts. He had no choice but to run. Perhaps Albany, he thought. He could disappear in Albany and maybe even find some work. On the way out of town, he would make a quick stop at the farmhouse and get his things. Rebecca would be happy to see him leave. Lost in thought as he crossed the hotel lobby, John calculated that he would have to rise early the next morning. No beer tonight, he thought. Well, maybe one or two.

When he climbed the stairs, John didn't notice the lone gentleman in the corner of the dining room. The well-dressed man, eating a fine steak dinner, enjoyed an almost perfect view of the hotel lobby. When he spotted John Wells, the man's head jerked up and the cup he held fell to the table. John Wells ignored the clatter of broken china and did not look back. Edgar Putnam breathed a sigh of relief.

Chapter 24

Tempting Death

Rebecca put the sleeping child in her bedroom and surrounded the infant with pillows and blankets on the off chance that the baby would roll over.

She searched the farmhouse, retrieving Isaac's shotgun and placing that too in her bedchamber. Next, she walked to the barn, and after a short conversation with Lucas sat at the kitchen table, considering her next move. She got up and jammed one of the kitchen chairs against the doorknob, because the lock didn't work. An intruder, like John, would make some noise she thought, before gaining access. After a restless evening and a mostly sleepless night, she rose early, fed the child, and sipped at her second cup of coffee when she noticed a lone man walking toward the farm. She recognized John's gait, ran to the bedroom and retrieved the shotgun. Rebecca waited for her unwanted visitor to reach the porch steps. She flung the chair to one side, threw open the door, and leveled the weapon at John's chest.

"That's far enough."

"This is my house. You got no right to stop me."

"This shotgun says otherwise."

"I'm leaving town; I gotta pack my things."

"I'll send the stuff to you. But you're not coming in this house. Now, if I were you, I'd get on your horse and ride out of here. The sheriff and the Army are looking for you."

John spat on the ground and scowled at his sister-in-law.

"This ain't right."

Rebecca pulled both hammers back on the shotgun and adjusted her aim.

"Get out of here. Now!"

She watched as John walked to the horse pasture, retrieved his mare and disappeared into the barn for the saddle. John stared at Rebecca one more time, mounted his horse and rode off at full gallop. Rebecca remained on the porch with the shotgun in her hands, until her evil brother-in-law became a small dot on the horizon.

Breathing easier, she went about her business, saving the outside chores for when the baby slept and wishing Lucas was still on hand to help. But, it being Sunday, Lucas got the day off. By mid-afternoon, she decided on a cup of tea and some sunshine for baby Isaac. She watched the little boy smile and gurgle his pleasure, clearly enjoying himself in the makeshift crib which she had fashioned from an old wooden crate. Rebecca made a mental note to invest in a proper crib for the baby when the tea kettle screamed for her attention. She returned to the porch less than a minute later. The baby was gone.

"He's a cute little thing, isn't he?"

John Wells, on the porch and smiling, held the baby to his chest with both arms. Rebecca lunged in his direction.

"Don't take another step woman or I'm gonna throw this little bastard into the well."

She froze in place.

"I don't have a lot of time. I want all of your money and my clothes, and you can bring me that shotgun too."

"Please, John, I'll do whatever you want. But don't hurt the baby."

"I'll wring his neck like a chicken, if you don't get movin."

Rebecca rushed through the farmhouse, grabbed an old carpet bag and shoved John's clothes and possessions into it, as fast as she could. She reached for the shotgun on her way out, remembering it was still loaded. The thought of using it crossed her mind, but only for an instant, Isaac was still in danger.

"Now that's more like it," said John.

"Please, give me the baby."

John wore his familiar sneer.

"You've come a long way, Rebecca. First, you couldn't wait to dump the little bastard, and now you're treating him like he was your own kid."

"Please, John, please give me the baby."

Rebecca stopped pleading, her eyes focused on the road. Three riders, maybe four, raised a large cloud of dust behind them. The two riders in the lead wore blue uniforms. John threw the baby in Rebecca's direction as he skipped down the stairs and off the porch. She fell to her knees and caught the baby with outstretched arms. She examined the boy but found no evidence of injury. Rebecca watched, as John scaled the rail fence and ran behind the barn, hiding from the soldiers, his horse apparently on the other side. John didn't know that the bull, relocated last week, now claimed that pasture as his own. The monstrous creature, like most bulls, charged anything that moved quickly but John took no notice. When the bull made contact, just one shake of the animal's horned head sent John into the air like a ragdoll. When the bull circled and charged again, John didn't move, and the animal stopped short. Rebecca, unaware of John's fate, pointed the soldiers to where she last saw her brother-in-law. Sheriff Bromley and Edgar Putnam followed. They found him lying in a blood-soaked patch of grass, his back and head supported by a fence post. A gaping wound, from the man's thigh to his groin exposed an ugly mass of muscle, ligaments, and bone. John did not acknowledge his captors, but focused, instead, on the tiny fountain of blood that squirted from his upper leg.

The soldiers and Bromley stopped short and looked away.

Putnam fell to his knees.

"John."

"I sure could use a beer right about now," John whispered.

Putnam reached for a bloody hand. John's head then fell to one side, his eyes half open.

"John?" said Putnam.

But John didn't answer.

Isaac looked forward to his next skirmish with the rebels.

His awkward fear had vanished, replaced with a reckless daring. He contemplated the unexpected change in his attitude while cleaning his rifle and putting an extra fine point on the bayonet. Isaac never considered himself a courageous soul and freedom for the slaves did not motivate him. Even President Lincoln fell victim to Isaac's transformation, the boy no longer inspired by a commander-in-chief who, like every other politician, played word games with other people's lives. *Whatever happened to that innocent farm boy from Keeseville*, he asked himself. He unholstered his sidearm, disassembled the weapon, and cleaned the pieces. As he commiserated the loss of his innocence, Isaac attacked the disassembled pistol with a fury, scrubbing each component with an oily rag until it glistened, like the sweat on his brow.

Isaac seethed with anger. *Life happened*, he concluded. The boy's dream of law school and a happy future with Rebecca was gone. The older brother he tried so hard to love betrayed him not once but repeatedly. The woman he loved also betrayed him, choosing to relive her past rather than embrace their future. The premature death of his friends and losing his father made Isaac an orphan, abandoned and alone. Isaac felt cheated. Cheated by the people he loved and cheated by the circumstances of his miserable existence. As a result, he didn't care anymore. He had but one task in life and that was to kill rebels. The same rebels who killed his friends directly or indirectly; the same rebels that were trying to kill him.

He pointed the spotless revolver at an imaginary, gray uniform on the horizon, eased the hammer back, and then pulled the trigger. The loud click, but no explosion, a symbol for his life, a meaningless and trivial occurrence about which no one knew or cared. Isaac thought about his new life as a soldier, wondering about his chances of survival. It didn't matter.

He no longer cared.

Rebecca adamantly opposed a church service for her late brother-in-law.

She insisted that Reverend Hagar appear at the gravesite and nothing more. The burial took place at the village cemetery on the Wells' family plot, John next to his father but Rebecca wondering if such a man could ever rest in peace. Hagar thought otherwise and dutifully recited the committal prayers. Rebecca, walked to her waiting carriage by the sheriff and Mr. Putnam, John's only mourners, turned to acknowledge their kindness.

The sheriff said his goodbyes; Putnam lingered.

"Have you heard from Isaac?" he asked.

"No, nothing. But I will write to him again. He must be told about John."

"What are you going to do, Rebecca?"

"I have no choice, Mr. Putnam. I will run the farm, with the two hired hands."

"But the baby, surely you. . ."

She interrupted her friend.

"Mr. Putnam, I am not the first woman who has been left alone because of this awful war. And I won't be the last. I'll manage."

Rebecca reached for Putnam and embraced him.

"Thank you. You have been very kind to my husband and me. I am most grateful."

Putnam tipped his hat and turned to leave.

Rebecca entered the empty farmhouse, little Isaac with Mrs. Lobdell once again, and set pen to paper immediately.

My dearest Isaac

I pray to God this letter finds you alive and well, for it has been much too long since I last received word from my brave husband.

I am forced to inform you of your brother's passing. An accident occurred on the farm and John succumbed to his injuries. John is resting in peace near your beloved father and I cherish the thought that we will soon be together again and pay our respects to both. I will manage the farm until you return.

Your loving wife,
Rebecca

Rebecca reread her words and winced that she could so easily, and without contrition, author such an incomplete narrative. She justified the letter by telling herself that Isaac did not deserve the pain and suffering that came with an accurate description of past events. The Rebecca of yesterday did not pen those words, she thought. She no longer had the luxury of mourning the dead or crying over the past. The farm and baby Isaac demanded that she grow up and move on.

The virgin bride had lost her innocence.

Chapter 25

Healing

In the weeks and months which followed the battle at Suffolk, Isaac's regiment moved on to Antioch Church, Baker's Crossroads, and Franklin. Each stop placed them closer to Richmond, Virginia.

When they reached the South Anna Bridge, the regiment marched under constant fire, in the face of a retreating enemy. Rebel pickets forced Isaac's company to seek temporary shelter in a small patch of trees. Isaac took cover in the ditch near the woods, with an open field in front of him. The company, with only a short time to regroup, then formed a straight line to prepare for an all-out assault on the rebel pickets, now scattered in the small trees and brush that lay ahead of the open field. The rebels, badly outnumbered, faced an onslaught. The charge sounded, and Isaac scrambled from the safety of his ditch. As he ran into the open field, having yet to fire his Enfield, Isaac felt a stabbing pain in his left arm. The bullet's impact sent the boy-soldier spinning in a counter clockwise direction. He fell backward, now facing the invasion of Union troops, but still in a sitting position. The young recruit watched, as the stain of red on his sleeve just above the elbow, grew in size. The whizzing noise of Minié balls as they flew past his head did not prompt the boy to run for cover. His sergeant, on one knee beside him, stopped long enough to render some medical advice.

"You'd better tie that off, Son, or you're gonna bleed to death."

And then he ran off.

Isaac used the leather strap on his haversack to fashion a crude tourniquet. He reached for his rifle and stood, unable to point the weapon, his left arm now useless. As he looked around, most of the Union troops disappeared into the thicket at the other end of the open field, a clear sign that the rebels retreated once again. With his rifle in one hand and the other arm swinging wildly at his side, Isaac walked toward the enemy.

A lone horse and wagon carrying two, other wounded soldiers, pulled alongside.

"Hop in," said the ambulance driver, we've got a surgeon and a hospital tent about one mile back."

Isaac nodded to his wounded compatriots, studying their wounds as he did so. The soldier in front of the wagon, and he was just a kid thought Isaac, had a head wound. His bloody bandage covered one eye, the remaining eye, bloodshot and unmoving. But for an occasional blink, Isaac thought the young soldier dead. The second soldier, also in pain, screamed with every bump of the slow-moving wagon. The bottom half of his right leg was nearly severed and rested at a right angle to his good leg, and was clearly damaged beyond repair.

The head wound said nothing, and Isaac looked away, studying the slow-moving terrain.

After the graveside service, Rebecca sat down with the hired hands.

They filed into the kitchen as she poured three cups of coffee, the two men different in every respect. George kept his gray hair short, said little, and said even less about the injury that left him with a limp, many years ago. He wore a deep tan, the standard uniform for one who spent a lifetime in the fields, and devoted hours tending to the farm animals, preferring the cows and horses to people. Abraham Wells hired the man and said he had a good feeling about

George. So did Rebecca. George worked hard and could be trusted to plow the fields, tend to the animals, and cut timber, without supervision. Being from the old school, George removed his hat when he sat at the kitchen table.

Lucas Alcott, the exact opposite of George, celebrated his sixteenth birthday, just one month ago. The boy attempted to enlist when he was fifteen, but the Union Army said no. John hired Lucas after the old man died. The kid and his dirt-poor family were dependent on the wages Lucas earned and joining the Army became impossible. If the boy went to war, his family could starve. Lucas, quick to smile, talked nonstop and often made rash decisions. When he talked too much, George groaned, rolled his eyes and shook his head. Sometimes it worked. On other occasions, George simply told the boy to shut up. Lucas took a quick liking to Rebecca that bordered on an adolescent crush. The boy, too shy to do or say anything about his feelings, used the baby, Isaac, as an excuse to hang around the farmhouse when the chores were done. Rebecca didn't object. Lucas, visibly nervous as he nibbled at the muffins which Rebecca baked that morning, blurted his guilty thoughts.

"I put the bull out to pasture cuz George told me to and because it was that time of the year, be'in that it was spring an all. I'm truly sorry about what happened. I just don't understand what John was doing out there in the first place."

Rebecca held her hand up.

"That's enough. We're not here to talk about John."

"Sorry for your loss, ma'am," said George.

"Thank you, thank you both."

Rebecca explained to the men she intended to keep the farm, maybe even expand it. She pointed out that she needed them more than ever and announced that each would be receiving a dollar more every week. Lucas, unable to restrain himself, babbled incessantly.

"Thank you, Miss Rebecca, I mean Mrs. Wells, you're generous, and you're beautiful, and gosh I don't know what to say. A whole dollar, my folks are gonna be real happy, and I was."

George groaned and rolled his eyes.

"Lucas, enough!"

Lucas stopped talking, and Rebecca pulled up a chair at the small table, leaned forward, and cupped her coffee in both hands.

"Now I want you, men, to tell me what we have to do to get this place in shape and make a good profit."

George looked at Lucas and removed the boy's hat.

"I'll do the talking, kid. You listen."

Lucas blushed and reached for another muffin.

Isaac's unblinking gaze betrayed his fear as the horse-drawn ambulance pulled alongside the hospital tent.

The assistant surgeon approached the buckboard and instructed his aides to remove the soldier with the head wound.

"Nothing I can do for him, put 'em next to the trees, with the two chest wounds." Isaac rose to his feet and stepped off the wagon, taking care not to jar his bloodied and broken arm. The assistant looked at the wound and shook his head.

"You, take a seat on that bench over there. There's two ahead of you."

Isaac walked slowly into the shade of the tent looking all around as he did so. The soldier with the shattered leg was carried in next.

"He goes to the head of the line," said the assistant.

The man with the disfigured leg did not react, his limb now attached with no more than a patch of skin. He appeared unconscious and didn't move. Isaac surveyed the scene around him as he waited for his turn with the doctors. A small mountain of severed arms, legs and feet lay less than a few yards from the shelter. The hundreds of flies buzzing around the bloody pile scattered when the surgeon's assistant threw another leg onto the heap. The sight and sound of dead flesh slapping into more dead flesh made Isaac queasy. He swallowed hard and resisted the urge to vomit.

The surgeon, covered in blood and clearly exhausted, yelled 'next' and the unconscious leg wound was brought to the operating table. The assistant reached for the chloroform and an oversized cotton ball.

"Don't bother; he's out. But we have to move quickly," said the surgeon.

Isaac watched, as did the dozen soldiers and officers who surrounded the operating theatre, mesmerized by the procedure. The doctor made several slices into the flesh to prepare for the amputation. He then scraped a portion of the bone clean and after double-checking his work, looked to the assistant, and produced a carpenter's saw. In seconds, another limb hit the pile. The unconscious soldier was moaning as the surgeon pulled a flap of skin over the open wound and sutured it with thread made from horse hair. The assistant surgeon, watched closely, as if still in training.

"I'm not going to suture the entire opening. You must leave a small hole for drainage," said the senior surgeon.

The assistant nodded his approval and turned to Isaac as two aides removed the one-legged victim.

"Next."

Isaac rose, walked slowly, but stopped well short of the surgeon's table.

"I've got a Minié ball stuck in my arm. Can you get it out?" he asked.

"Sorry, Son, the arm's gotta go," said the surgeon.

The assistant reached for Isaac's good arm and urged him closer.

"No, you're not going to take my arm. Just get that bullet out and patch me up."

The surgeon wiped the sweat off his brow and then used the same bloody rag to get the blood and bone matter out of his long beard. He also wiped his crimson colored hands. When finished, he tossed the dirty towel into a basin filled with pink water. An aide rinsed it and hung it out to dry on one of the tent's anchor ropes.

"Listen to me, Boy. A wound like that can lead to hospital gangrene or if you're lucky, the fever. Either way, you're likely to die unless we amputate. Now get on the table."

Isaac pulled his Colt revolver and held it just inches from the assistant surgeon's face. He eased the hammer back, and everyone within earshot stopped breathing. Isaac didn't have to raise his voice, the click from his weapon spoke volumes.

"You patch me up, or I'll blow his brains all over this place."

The surgeon let his head droop and reached for a small scalpel.

"Where in tarnation are they getting these new recruits?" he asked no one in particular.

Isaac refused to move, the assistant surgeon wide-eyed and shaking uncontrollably.

"We'll do it your way," said the surgeon. "Have a seat."

Isaac lost consciousness during the painful effort to remove the Minié ball from his arm.

He refused the anesthetic for fear that the surgeon might take advantage of his unconscious state and sever the boy's arm. Isaac worried and suffered for no reason.

"I'm not a butcher."

The voice, sitting at the end of Isaac's cot, belonged to the senior surgeon. Still groggy, Isaac carefully examined the bandage which now covered his upper arm. He could move his thumb, but the fingers failed to respond.

"Thank you," said Isaac.

"Pyemia."

"What's that?" asked Isaac.

"Pus in the blood. There's a good chance you're going to get it, plus the fever."

"What do I do?"

"I'm in no position to be changing bandages every day, but you should, as often as you can. Rinse the wound with water, whiskey, if you got it. Try to keep it clean and don't be afraid to let the air get to it. Not sure what any of that does, but sometimes it helps."

The doctor stood up, tugged at his beard, and put out his hand.

"We do the best we can," he said, an air of apology in his voice.

Isaac returned the surgeon's gesture.

"Tell your assistant, I'm sorry."

The bearded man laughed.

"He's still jawing about it. Says he almost bought the farm."

"I was bluffing," said Isaac.

The surgeon went back to his tent and Isaac, now focused on his bandaged arm, mumbled to himself.

"I wasn't bluffing."

Isaac changed his bandage every day for three days. He woke up on the fourth day struggling to get off his cot, suffering from the cold sweats and a burning forehead. The predicted fever had arrived. One of the aides came by occasionally and offered Isaac some water. When Isaac complained about his loose bowels, they gave him opium. The liquid form, known as laudanum, did not stop diarrhea, it made the boy even weaker. After two more days with the same symptoms, Isaac walked and crawled to the surgeon's tent.

"Please, you gotta help me," Isaac whispered, leaning against the tent pole for support.

The surgeon, just waking from a badly needed rest, pulled the bandage off Isaac's arm.

"No gangrene. That's good."

He reached for a wooden crate under his bed and returned to Isaac's side with a small bottle of whiskey, half empty.

"Drink this, all of it."

Isaac did as he was told and began a minute-long, coughing spell.

"Now get down to the creek."

"Swim?" asked Isaac, incredulous at the surgeon's suggestion.

"I don't care if you sit, stand, or swim. Keep your clothes on and stay in that water for as long as you can stand it. You're burning up, and the water will cool you down. Who knows, maybe the fever will break. Now, I gotta go, more wounded."

Isaac, emboldened by the whiskey, stumbled his way to the creek, several hundred yards away. He stayed in the cold water for more than an hour, fully clothed and shivering. But his fever subsided, and it was either the alcohol or the frigid water that propelled him back to his cot, sleepy but feeling better. He slept for twelve hours. When he woke, his arm still throbbed but the fever had disappeared. This time he walked with purpose to the water, removed his bandage, and soaked the sore arm until his skin was wrinkled. He remained on sick call for a few more days, his wound slowly healing. Although, still sore, it seemed to heal nicely.

"Wells, you got mail."

Isaac bolted to a sitting position, glanced at the sergeant, but focused his stare on the envelope.

"Yes, sir," said Isaac, with a smile and a salute.

"We're headed out to Yorktown in a few days. You feel up to traveling?"

"I'll be at roll call tomorrow morning, sir, I promise," said Isaac, eyeing the letter still in the sergeant's hand.

"Enjoy the letter, but I'm counting on you, Wells. Understand?"

"Yes, sir."

Isaac grabbed the letter, ripping the envelope and tossing it aside, instantly recognizing Rebecca's handwriting. He forced himself to read the lines, twice, hoping that he made some sort of mistake. Isaac rose from the cot and stared at the words again. There was no mistake. John was dead. The boy collapsed onto the cot and sat there, using both hands to cradle his head. The letter fluttered to the ground.

He didn't weep for his dead brother. Instead, Isaac's stomach churned with guilt and relief, panic and then calm–the man who caused him so much pain and grief, now dead. He forced himself to recollect happier times when the two siblings worked and played as friends. He also thought of Rebecca–alone on the farm and unable to manage. Still angry, he crumpled the letter and threw it away.

Chapter 26

A Stranger

Little Isaac, now five months old, continued to cry.

George took a rare day off, with severe pain in his bad leg, and Lucas seemed to be knocking at Rebecca's door every five minutes. Rebecca could not recall a more difficult morning on the farm.

"Lucas, if I see you at my door one more time, I'm gonna shoot you," she said, after yet another knock.

"Mrs. Wells."

Rebecca turned abruptly, verifying first, that her shotgun was near the door. The man on her porch, at least six feet tall, wore a dark grey, John Bull hat with a dark suit and carried a walking stick, with an ivory handle. He wore a vest under his jacket, a white shirt with a black bowtie and a gold chain draped from one pocket to the next. His boots, being cleaned and polished, made his big, red bulbous nose the only part of his appearance that looked out of place.

"Yes," she replied, the distinct smell of alcohol making her move one step closer to the shotgun.

"Mrs. Wells, my name is Victor Calhoun. I'd like to talk to you about your farm."

"I don't understand."

"I'm willing to take it off your hands."

"My farm is not for sale."

Rebecca attempted to close the door, but Calhoun wedged his foot in the doorway. "Mrs. Wells, I know for a fact that your brother-in-law is dead. Your husband signed up for three years, you haven't heard from him, and he's probably dead too. A girl like you has no place running a farm. I'm willing to give you a fair price."

Rebecca reached for the shotgun but chose not to point the weapon at the stranger, pretending to inspect the barrel instead.

"Mr. Calhoun, I'll say it again. This farm is not for sale. Please leave."

Calhoun removed his foot from the door and was forced to shout his response.

"I already own half the farms on the road to Port Kent. You'll sell out. It's just a matter of time."

Rebecca slammed the door shut and moved to the kitchen window, watching the man as he mounted his horse and trotted off.

Rebecca wondered if her bad day just grew worse.

The 118th Regiment welcomed Isaac with news of yet another march.

They covered familiar ground, a twenty-two-mile hike for the train that deposited the men in Norfolk. The steamer, *Utica,* then transported the soldiers past Fort Monroe, and on to Yorktown. Several regiments gathered in Yorktown, and the rumor quickly spread that a move on Petersburg could be next.

Isaac recalled his history, as more troops arrived, Yorktown being the scene where Lord Cornwallis surrendered to George Washington in 1781. Most of the troops, ignorant of the history which surrounded them, jumped into the York River to cool off. They also entertained themselves by teasing their camp sutler, caught selling prohibited whiskey, and forced to ride the "wooden horse," a twelve-foot-high monstrosity made entirely of rough-hewn, wooden planks. Besides the physical pain, the sutler suffered acute embarrassment when hundreds of laughing soldiers stopped to laugh or comment on the errant man's predicament.

The mood of the men turned somber when, at three in the morning, the soldiers of both the 118th and the NY 99th received orders to leave bag and baggage in the camp and proceed forthwith to the river. The troops boarded the steamer, *Keuka,* and by the next day, reached White House. This was not the executive mansion in Washington DC but rather the site of a dilapidated mansion where George Washington once courted Martha. More importantly, White House was the name given to that spot on the map where the Richmond and New York Railroad crossed the Pamunkey River. A series of incomplete rebel fortifications served as a reminder that it could have been a major staging area for Confederate weapons and supplies.

Isaac and his colleagues set up their dog tents in a nearby cornfield and slept soundly, despite a pouring rain. Although soaked to the skin, no one bothered to dry their uniforms as the rain continued for most of the day. That evening, Isaac and a handful of his comrades formed an advanced picket. After crossing the river in the dark, they occupied a small hamlet. Encountering no resistance, they invited the balance of their regiments to join them. On the next day, July 4, the men marched twenty-five miles, in hot and dusty conditions, to Hanover Junction. The rail line to Richmond crossed the Virginia Central Railroad at this point, and Confederate supplies from the Shenandoah Valley came through here. Whoever controlled the junction also controlled most of northern Virginia. Several buildings, still burning from a previous skirmish, served as a reminder that the Confederate army continued to lurk nearby, although in temporary retreat.

As the men rested from their long march, Isaac and several other men, received a new assignment. They would test the enemy's strength with a small skirmishing party, sent under cover of darkness. The dangerous mission weighed heavily on their minds and the men, desperate to occupy the hours until darkness, discovered an abandoned corn mill. After some quick repairs and a trip to a cornfield, the men produced a large quantity of cornmeal. They concocted a hot pudding with the cornmeal, and several men feasted on their first, hot, meal in days.

Isaac wondered if it would be his last meal.

"Good morning, Gentlemen."

The dozen men who regularly hosted Abraham Wells in a back room at the general store scrambled to their feet. The scrape of chairs on the hardwood floor, along with the noise of throats being cleared, made Rebecca grin.

"I hope I'm not disturbing you."

Murmurs and a few mumbled greetings did not stop Rebecca from pursuing her mission.

"My late father-in-law spoke very highly of your gatherings."

After a short period of stunned silence, one old farmer stepped forward.

"Please, Mrs. Wells, won't you sit down."

Several men scurried to provide a chair, several more removed their hats and pocketed their pipes.

"I've come here on business," said Rebecca.

She recounted the ominous proposal from Victor Calhoun and repeated her refusal to sell the farm.

"Mr. Calhoun claims to have a number of converts here in Essex County. I would like to know your feelings in this regard," said Rebecca.

Most of the men nodded and several admitted to discussing such things with Calhoun.

"So, am I to conclude that Mr. Calhoun has persuaded some of you to sell out?"

Again, the room was quiet. After a moment, the same gentleman who invited her to sit down, leaned forward in his chair, wringing his hat as he focused on the young woman.

"I will soon be seventy years old. I have no family to speak of and no one to inherit my farm. Mr. Calhoun has approached me, and I am considering his offer."

The old farmer sat back and fixed his gaze on a knothole in the plank floor.

"I will purchase your farm," said Rebecca.

Several men snickered; several more frowned and spoke under their breath. One of them spoke up.

"Little girl, you got no business operating a farm, now why don't you head on home."

Rebecca ignored the unsolicited advice and rose to her feet. She turned to the aging farmer, but her remarks were for everyone in the room.

"Farms have a way of getting bigger or smaller. The big ones survive. The small ones get smaller and then they die," she said, waiting for her remarks to sink in.

"Your friend, Abraham Wells, told me that, a long time ago. I never forgot it. Neither should any of you."

She stepped forward and placed her hand on the retiring farmer's shoulder.

"My place is on the road to Port Kent. We should talk."

As Rebecca exited, her audience rose to its feet once again. A few said good bye, but most said nothing, scratching their heads and reaching for their pipes.

Chapter 27

Sneak Attack

It didn't take long for the skirmishers to encounter Confederate pickets.

When the loud report of rifles commenced and Minié balls whizzed by, the Union soldiers dropped to the ground and lay as flat as they could, reduced to firing at the enemy's rifle flashes, it being a cloudy night and the half moon offering only occasional assistance. The troops on both sides of Isaac's company encountered the same resistance. When they fell back and reported to their superiors, everyone agreed that the bridge over the Pamunkey river was well guarded.

After a sleepless night, the soldiers' anxieties now confirmed, preparations for an immediate battle began shortly after daybreak. Union troops, approximating the meandering path of the river, headed north to the Hanover Courthouse. They took up the Virginia Central rail tracks as far as they could, and in both directions. They also destroyed the trestle which crossed the main road. Union soldiers then attacked the bridge, with a full complement of over 1,100 men plus artillery. The eighty Confederate troops guarding the bridge held out for an hour and then retreated or surrendered, depending on their ability to escape. After firing upon the bridge, Union troops pushed further in pursuit of the enemy but were delayed by a fleeing resident who cautioned Union officers that an entire Confederate Brigade was lying in wait at Hanover Junction. The men in blue, disappointed they would not be going onto Richmond, marched back to their base camp. Isaac received a message to report to the corporal.

"You and Nicholson are going with me on a moonlight stroll this evening. We need to confirm the whereabouts of that brigade, if it exists at all," said the corporal.

"Any questions?"

"No, sir," said Isaac.

It made no sense to linger at White House Landing, so the men walked the short distance to Cash Corners, just three miles north. A small, wooded area gave the men some cover as they walked slowly in a northerly direction. While the half moon made their hike less difficult, the men became visible targets for the enemy.

The corporal motioned and then stopped abruptly. Isaac and Private Nicholson did the same, standing perfectly still as their officer cautioned them, with a finger to his lips, to make no noise. Isaac could hear the rustle of bushes to his north. The three men pointed their Enfield rifles in that direction. But there was more noise on their left and seconds later, on their right. The three soldiers closed ranks, each facing in a different direction, with back to friendly back. The rustling noise stopped.

"Are you fellows lost?"

The shouted query from somewhere in the trees made Isaac jump but neither he nor his two comrades dared to move, peering instead behind every tree.

"I count three of you, and I reckon there's about forty of us. What say you put those guns on the ground real slow like?"

Isaac looked to the corporal for guidance. The officer hesitated and rifle clicks, as loud as thunder to the three trapped men, settled the matter. Nicholson did not wait for the order, stooped to place his rifle on the ground in front of him and then removed his sidearm with the opposite hand. The cautious soldier did not want to startle his enemies. The corporal nodded, his eyes downcast, as he too placed his weapons on the ground. Isaac followed suit, but he had not drawn his Colt revolver when five Confederate soldiers stepped out from the trees. One, gray uniform approached Isaac, grinning.

"You ain't too smart, Boy."

Isaac, angry and embarrassed by the rebels' successful bluff, grew red in the face and instinctively reached for his sidearm. The rebel used the butt of his rifle as a club, smashing it into the side of Isaac's head. Isaac fell to the ground, a three-inch gash on his cheekbone spurting blood. The gray uniform thrust his rifle downward; its bayonet now inches from Isaac's throat.

"Like I said, Boy, you ain't too smart."

Isaac raised his head and tried to speak, but everything went black.

After spending the night at her mother's boarding house, Mrs. Lobdell wanted time with baby Isaac, Rebecca got an early start on the trip back to the Wells family farm.

The baby, going on seven months, was growing in strength and already demonstrated a personality of his own. As the horse-drawn buckboard slowly approached the farmhouse, Rebecca contemplated her progress since Isaac's departure. She smiled when her thoughts drifted back to the general store and wondered whether the retiring farmer would consider her offer. She had the funds for a significant down payment and could easily afford the mortgage. George and Lucas were good workers and could easily handle two locations. But clearly, the men were not comfortable with a woman in their midst, much less their livelihood.

As she congratulated herself, a frown crossed her face. The fence, which marked the north property line, lay on the ground, cross rails and posts strewn over the side of the road. As she approached the farmhouse, Rebecca noted several hogs out of their pen and in her garden. Several chickens lay dead on her porch and a number of the farmhouse windows were now shattered, their clean white curtains billowing in the wind.

She pulled the buckboard to a stop and rushed to the house, with Isaac in her arms. Both George and Lucas were sitting at the kitchen table. Each stood, yet downcast and silent, and removed their hats, when Rebecca stormed into the room. She stopped, the baby still in her arms, fear in her eyes."

"What happened?"

George did the talking, Lucas–unusually quiet.

"We got here early this morning to do the chores. I figure it happened last night, while you were gone."

Rebecca did not want the men to see the fear in her heart, but she saw no reason to disguise her anger or smother her unladylike response.

"The bastards that did this will pay for it.

"Have you been in the barn?" asked George.

"No, why?"

"They killed two of the cows. Slit their throats."

Rebecca staggered to the rocking chair that no one, except John, had dared sit in since the death of her father-in-law. She pretended to fuss over the child but rocked back and forth at an increasingly furious pace. When she stopped, a single tear rolling down one cheek, she used the sleeve on her dress to wipe her face. The Rebecca that rose from Abraham's rocking chair no longer resembled the Rebecca that ran from her fears and hid from the awful memories of her past. She took a deep breath, and then turned in their direction.

"No one is going to chase me off my own farm. Fix the fence, get those hogs back in their pen, and save as much meat as you can from the cows and the chickens. Get things right before dark, today, and I'll pay you extra. I'll talk to the sheriff tomorrow."

Lucas stepped forward, repeatedly striking his leg with the rolled up hat he had been wringing with his hands.

"This ain't right, ma'am. We'll fix things up like they was before and we don't need no money, do we, George?"

George pressed his lips into a straight line.

"No, Lucas, we don't need the money."

Lucas threw his arm over George's shoulder, and the two men left. Rebecca put the baby to bed, returned to the kitchen, and loaded her shotgun–both barrels.

Isaac needed help from the corporal and Private Nicholson as he climbed into the boxcar.

The three prisoners were not alone, over two dozen blue uniforms waited their turn and allowed the wounded to board first. Isaac's bandage, now soaked with blood, covered the nasty cut he received at the hands of a rebel soldier. It did nothing for the pain from his broken cheekbone.

The Virginia Central Railroad ran due south from the Hanover Courthouse. The twenty-mile journey would take at least an hour, and there would be no stops for a bathroom much less, a hot meal. A corner of the box was designated as a latrine, and several men scoured the interior of their prison-on-wheels for a way out. The absence of loose boards and large holes prevented an escape and choked off their supply of fresh air.

Most men predicted that a prison in Richmond would be their new home–Belle Isle, Castle Thunder, and Libby Prison, all mentioned. Each owned a reputation for harsh conditions including no food, widespread sickness, and cruel treatment. Some men used cracks in the side of the walls to guess their final destination, and one soldier spied warehouses alongside the James River. Libby Prison became the consensus choice as the prisoners' new home.

After the train slowed to a halt, the boxcar went silent. Eyes shut tight when the sliding door opened; the Virginia sun temporarily blinding the prisoners.

"Everyone out," barked the guard.

The inmates tumbled out, and Isaac leaned heavily on his corporal and Nicholson to accomplish the four-foot drop without falling.

"Officers over there, the rest of you mongrels can line up right here."

Nicholson looked at the corporal.

"Go," he said.

But the corporal hung onto Isaac, placing his hat on the boy's head.

"You're a corporal now."

Isaac was in too much pain to object and dutifully followed his commanding officer.

"Keep your mouth shut; I'll do the talking."

"Name and rank," said the burly man in gray.

He was standing near another gray uniform, a mousy looking fellow, bespectacled and writing furiously, his makeshift desk, a single barrel.

"Charles Porter, Corporal."

Porter waited for the clerk to finish writing and jerked his head toward Isaac.

"He can't talk, one of your men broke his jaw. His name is Isaac Wells. He's a corporal."

The burly man stepped closer and studied Isaac's coat.

"Don't look like no corporal to me."

Isaac tried to focus on his captor, but it was difficult. He remembered that Libby Prison was for officers only, glanced at the guard, and then deliberately collapsed at his feet.

"Oh hell, he's gonna be dead inside a week anyway. Get 'em outa here. Now!"

Porter pulled and dragged Isaac out of the guard's view. As they waited in the officers' line, the two men got their first up-close look at Libby Prison. The three-story structure, formally a warehouse, commanded a major portion of the James River waterfront. The massive building, actually three separate buildings, occupied an entire city block on tobacco road–on one side of the prison, Cary Street, on the other side, the James River. The walls of the building were whitewashed so as to highlight anyone foolish enough to linger near the prison. The windows on the second and third floors were barred and open offering scant protection from the harsh winters and blistering summers of Richmond, Virginia.

Isaac watched, as the enlisted men were formed into a long line and force marched past the prison in a westerly direction.

"Belle Isle is my guess," said Porter, speculating as to the men's final destination.

"Move it."

The order to enter the building was shouted by another guard, his rifle pointing at the prisoners.

"Move it, I said," as he pushed a limping officer, struggling to keep up.

Isaac, surprised when he got past the first-floor entrance, surveyed a roomful of desks and a score of gray-uniformed men, but the inmates, ushered up two flights of stairs, discovered a third-floor, completely open and occupied by hundreds of men. The absence of beds forced every man present to sit or lie on the floor when he could no longer stand. Isaac and Porter found a place to sit in the far corner. They estimated that at least four hundred men were in the building but doubled that number when they traveled down to the second-floor kitchen. They stood in line for a small slice of cornbread, their only meal that day, but it didn't matter, the tales of woe from fellow prisoners had destroyed their appetites.

Prisoners who lingered too often or too long near the windows, barred with wooden dowels, received severe punishment, several of them, shot on sight. Medical attention for the sick and wounded rarely occurred, unless an imprisoned Union surgeon slipped into the building. The so-called hospital, on the first floor, consisted of a single room where only the seriously ill were brought, and then only to die. A basement referred to as Rat Hell, flooded and, except for the occasional black inmate, housed hundreds of hungry rats.

On a more cheerful note, the inmates received occasional permission to send a letter to family. A six-line limit made the exercise more frustrating than therapeutic. A prison newsletter called the *Libby Chronicle*, circulated among the captives, the hand-written document often passed around for anyone to read. Political beliefs repeatedly expressed in writing and during verbal exchanges on the prison floor, often took a hostile view of Abraham Lincoln, most inmates blaming the president because they had yet to be rescued.

"Has anyone ever escaped?" asked Isaac, his words muffled by a broken jawbone.

The small group of officers who had befriended Isaac and his corporal went silent. One soldier, wearing a captain's uniform, looked around as if someone might be listening or watching.

"Not yet," he said.

Chapter 28

Caution

"You be careful, Rebecca, this Calhoun feller is no gentleman."

Rebecca watched as Sheriff Bromley puffed on his pipe, sending a swell of smoke in her direction. He rose to his feet and paced. She stepped in his path and locked her eyes on his.

"I'm not backing down, Sheriff."

He turned away, stared at the office wall, and then turned back.

"I know what you're capable of Mrs. Wells."

He was warning her, Rebecca thought. Bromley did not want the woman to take matters into her own hands. Rebecca surprised herself and challenged the sheriff.

"Are you going to spend your nights at my farm?" she asked.

Bromley exhaled, threw his unlit pipe on the desk, and plopped into his chair.

"I'll give you one thing, Rebecca, you don't back down from a fight."

Rebecca sensed an opportunity and pressed the sheriff a bit more.

"If he's on my property, do I have the right to chase him off?"

The sheriff tugged on his mustache.

"Yes, but you can't kill a man for trespassing."

Rebecca stopped on her way to the door.

"I'll aim low."

"It's not healing."

The orderly removed the dirty, red-stained bandage from Isaac's head, revealing a mostly open wound and a great deal of swelling around the cheekbone. One week passed, since Isaac's confrontation with the Rebel soldier. The young farm boy shrugged his shoulders and stood up to leave.

"I'm not staying down here."

Isaac referred to the so-called hospital on the east side of the first floor, in the tobacco warehouse-turned prison. Soldiers who visited that small room never returned.

"I can stitch you up and give you a new bandage. But it's going to hurt, and we are all out of chloroform."

Isaac studied the hospital orderly who regularly worked without a doctor. Although a young man, he grew old, with large bags under his eyes, a thin, emaciated frame and a sadness in his brown eyes that made you look away, less the sadness be contagious. Isaac looked at the filthy bandage he held in his hands and focused on a nearby soldier, the man's head completely bandaged leaving the soldier blind but still able to moan from the pain.

"Let's get it over with," said Isaac.

Lieutenant Porter held Isaacs head still, while the orderly stabbed his face with a large needle, using it to pull a length of horse hair. Isaac counted twenty-six perforations for a total of thirteen stitches. The counting made the pain more bearable.

"The cut should heal, but if it gets red or starts oozing pus, you'll have to come back so I can lance it. The jawbone is broken, but you know that. Still hurt?"

Not as bad as it did, last week." said Isaac.

It's healing. Crooked I'm afraid. You will not be quite so handsome."

Isaac relieved that it was over and extremely fatigued, looked around at the small sea of bodies, many writhing and groaning in pain.

"They're a lot worse off than I am, Doc. They'll all be dead by the time Lincoln and his generals get off their ass."

"I'm not a doctor."

"That's all right; I'm not an officer."

Lieutenant Porter slapped Isaac on the shoulder.

"You've got a big mouth, Wells. That's what landed you here in the first place."

The orderly now focused on the genuine lieutenant, hesitated and reached for Porter's forehead with the back of his hand. Porter pushed it away. The orderly insisted. Porter complained.

"Nothing wrong with me, Doc."

"Your eyes are glassy, your face is flushed, and you're running a fever."

"Well, I've had the trots, since I got here. You got anything for that?"

The orderly shook his head, his eyes on the floor.

"You can die from dysentery down here."

Lieutenant Porter placed his hat on Isaac's now bandaged head.

"Come on, Lieutenant, we best get you back to our little corner of this hell hole."

The orderly reached for the dirty bandage.

"We can use that again."

Rebecca, still uneasy with the prospect of yet another visit by vandals, guided her horse and wagon in a northerly direction, toward Keeseville.

With baby Isaac visiting Mrs. Lobdell for the remainder of the week and both Lucas and George standing guard on the farm, Rebecca traveled alone to retrieve a month's worth of supplies. Her arduous work became easier when several men at the general store offered to load the wagon. Rebecca stared at the post office, a few minutes' walk from the store, took a few steps, changed her mind, and returned to the wagon, shaking her head.

"Damn you, Isaac."

The workers heard her language and picked up their pace. Rebecca turned back toward the post office thinking it was a waste of her time, but crossing the street anyway. The clerk recognized his young visitor.

"Good morning, Mrs. Wells."

He did not wear his usual frown, instead, he looked somber, Rebecca thought. The man produced an envelope even before Rebecca reached the counter. She grabbed the envelope but studied his face for a clue. Thrusting it quickly into her bag, she thanked the man, turned and walked with renewed determination, as if the workers had also loaded the solution to her worries. After climbing into the wagon but before the horses were asked to do their job, Rebecca retrieved the letter and stole a quick glance. Isaac did not send this letter; the handwriting looked different. She took a sharp breath, forced herself to calm down, and shoved the letter back into the cloth purse where it could not harm her. She snapped at the horses with the reins and reached the edge of the village when her discipline finally crumbled. Pulling the wagon to a halt, she reached for the bag and removed the envelope. Rebecca ripped it open and let the envelope flutter to the ground, both of her hands shaking and forcing the woman to grip the paper as if it might escape.

South Anna Bridge
July 10, 1863

To the family of Isaac Wells,

I regret to inform you that in a skirmish with enemy soldiers, Isaac Wells, along with his Lieutenant and a fellow soldier, was taken prisoner and, on this day, remains in enemy hands.

We believe he was unhurt and suspect that he has been transported to one of the several confederate prisons in the Richmond Virginia area.

Isaac has served his Regiment with great distinction and we pray for his safe return. I am very respectfully yours,

Cptn. William H. Bailey

Rebecca's face turned to stone. With mechanical precision, she folded the letter, and tucked it into her bag, careful to prevent any unwanted creases or wrinkles. The reins hit each horse with enough violence to lurch the team into a gallop. She slowed the animals, but only a little, creating a storm cloud of dust in her wake. George and Lucas waived as she pulled the wagon alongside the farmhouse, but she did not acknowledge their gesture, leaving them to unload the wagon as she disappeared from view. When she entered the kitchen, Rebecca removed her bonnet, threw her shawl on the Victorian sofa, and sat in the rocking chair. She rocked furiously, forcing the wooden floor to squeal like a cat in pain. Although overwhelmed with worry and pain, Rebecca did not cry. She refused to cry, the new Rebecca did not allow such indulgences. Her back and forth motion ceased as quickly as it had begun. She explained herself to the walls.

"I'm not giving up. I'm not giving up."

Isaac, tired and hungry, drifted off to sleep on his hard and unforgiving bed, a sliver of floor, in a rundown, tobacco warehouse.

A few minutes passed when a flailing arm slapped Isaac's broken cheekbone and sent the injured man into a painful frenzy.

"Lieutenant Porter, I've never hit an officer before but . . ."

The faint light, from a waning moon, exposed enough of Porter's face for Isaac to see the man's suffering. The lieutenant trembled from the cold but sweat enough to soak his shirt and drench his scalp. His forehead burned with fever and the man slipped in and out of delirium. Isaac pulled the lieutenant close into a bear hug, a clumsy attempt to keep Porter warm and a clear admission that he could do nothing more for the dying man. Isaac and his patient took turns sleeping until the sun's rays broke through the prison's windows. The fake lieutenant enlisted the help of a nearby soldier, and the two men struggled to deliver Porter to a bed in the prison hospital. The orderly, respectful but firm, delivered the bad news.

"All the beds are full, put the lieutenant on the floor in that corner, over there. Please."

The private looked after the lieutenant who once looked after the private. He did not leave the sick man's side. The orderly brought a small tin cup half-filled with water, Isaac used a portion to wet the man's lips, the balance used to soak a neckerchief and cool the man's forehead.

"It's the fever. There's not much we can do." said the orderly.

Isaac nodded his head, the orderly turned away, and the boy's thoughts drifted back to a happier time when he, his brother, and his parents attended Services as a family.

"My flesh and my heart may fail, but God is the strength of my heart and my portion forever."

Disgusted with himself for remembering such foolishness, Isaac scowled, cleared his nostrils with a long snort, and spat the results on a nearby wall. He focused instead on the windows and wondered whether he could break the wooden bars and escape. The orderly interrupted Isaac's fantasy with a small slice of cornbread.

"He's not going to eat that," Isaac said.

"It's for you."

Isaac nibbled at the stale bread, neither famished nor hungry because he knew that the lieutenant would soon affect an escape of his own to a "better place," according to the Reverend Hagar. *A bunch of bull,* thought Isaac. *Anything would be better than this hell hole.*

Porter lingered for two more days and nights. Isaac did not waiver, never leaving the lieutenant's side. During one of those times, when Isaac allowed himself a few hours of anxious sleep, Porter made his escape, slipping into the same black abyss that swallowed Isaac's father, brother, and too many of his friends. Isaac often thought of that nothingness and anticipated the end of his own suffering on this earth. He welcomed the relief that came with death and no longer feared the possibility. As he stared at the gray, lifeless form in his arms, it occurred to him that Rebecca was all that remained. But she lived in another world, never to be seen again. And so, he abandoned the memory of her face in his mind and focused on the dead man's face, instead.

"He's gone, sir."

It was the orderly, announcing the obvious.

Two soldiers removed the body, but Isaac thought to grab the rolled-up coat that had served as Porter's pillow for the last days of his life.

The imposter now wore a lieutenant's hat and coat.

Chapter 29

Teamwork

Rebecca woke to the sound of someone pounding on the farmhouse door.

She lit the lamp as quickly as she dared and raced to the banging noise, now frantic. The new key in the lock triggered a scream.

"Mrs. Wells, Mrs. Wells, come quick."

Lucas, who had agreed to spend his nights in the barn less Calhoun's thugs paid another visit, struggled to shout his news.

"Fire."

When she opened the door, she saw the reason for Lucas's panic–a hay wagon, adjacent to the barn, on fire.

"If we hitch the horse to the wagon we can . . ."

Rebecca waved her hand and shook her head.

"No time for that. We will be the horses."

They both ran to the burning wagon, picked up the tongue and leaned forward.

"It won't budge," yelled Lucas.

"Pull harder."

But the wagon refused to move, its flames licking the barn wall.

"Again," she screamed, the veins in her neck now showing and Lucas red-faced.

Lucas screamed in anguish, Rebecca yelled again.

"Pull hard."

The wagon moved forward, just inches, but enough to give them renewed hope.

"Keep pulling," she screamed.

The momentum increased and soon the wagon was a safe distance from the barn. Lucas turned and pointed.

"Look."

He pointed to the barn wall, now covered with gyrating yellow and orange devils, threatening to dance the barn into ashes. They ran for the well, Rebecca filling the bucket, Lucas making the mad dash to the barn and throwing the water where he hoped it would do the most good. She retrieved a second bucket, and Lucas now ran to and from the barn as fast as he could. After a series of trips, Lucas, soaking wet and exhausted, fell to his knees gasping for air.

"The flames are out."

Rebecca pointed.

"It's still smoldering."

"She filled a series of buckets, running back and forth, until she too fell onto her knees, coughing and struggling to catch her breath. When the smoke cleared, they examined the damage. The vertical studs were still intact, but half of the wall was no more than a sheet of black cinder. To be safe, most of the planking would have to be replaced.

"I'm sorry, Mrs. Wells. I was sleeping. I didn't hear a thing until they left. Sounded like one, maybe two riders."

Rebecca shook her head and used both of her hands to cradle Lucas's sweaty face. He was more than a head taller and only a few years younger, but Rebecca talked to the boy as if he were her son. "You did nothing wrong, Lucas. We saved the barn, thank the good Lord, we saved the barn."

Lucas, tears now mixing with sweat, hugged the woman. "I wanna kill the bastards, Mrs. Wells. I truly want to kill 'em."

Isaac, too, smoldered with anger and bitterness.

Union warehouses sent hundreds of boxes each week but none reached the prisoners. They watched, instead, as Confederate soldiers and desperate locals pillaged or simply removed entirely the foodstuffs and provisions intended for the cold and hungry occupants of Libby Prison.

The large gash on Isaac's face left an ugly scar and the broken cheekbone, although healed, left his face disfigured and misshapen. Although he had no access to a mirror, Isaac concluded from the constant stares that he no longer possessed the rugged good looks of his teen years. But the wounds that hurt the most were not visible, and the young soldier made no effort to hide his anger.

"Is my uniform gray?" Isaac asked.

Each time he approached the small group of officers near his sleeping spot on the floor, their conversation would come to an abrupt halt. They stared at Isaac as if he were a dangerous intruder.

"You're not an officer, are you?" said one of them.

"No. If I was an officer, I'd have a real, pretty face."

The man who challenged Isaac, a lieutenant, jumped to his feet and swung a closed fist in Isaac's direction. With little effort, the farm boy, still muscle-bound from his years in the fields, caught the man's fist in the palm of one hand. The loud slapping noise ended the nearby conversations, many prisoners now staring at Isaac and his would-be assailant. Isaac squeezed the man's fist making the genuine lieutenant wince. Isaac smiled.

"Don't do that again. You wouldn't want to hurt yourself."

Most of the soldiers, within earshot, chuckled, but not the lieutenant.

When Isaac released the man's fist, he reached back for a second attempt.

"Gentlemen, we're forgetting our manners."

The voice belonged to a colonel, and when he stood to greet Isaac, the others rose with him.

"Colonel Tom Rose. But I guess my 'eagles' don't mean much in a place like this.

Isaac studied the buttons on the colonel's coat. They glimmered in the light, almost new, their appearance not unlike the officer's boots.

"I guess colonels don't get dirty when someone else is doing the fighting for them," said Isaac.

The colonel bit his lip, his eyes looking down and focused on Isaac's worn and dirty boots.

"I was captured at Chickamauga. Escaped and then captured again."

Isaac jerked his head up, realizing that he might have been overly harsh.

"I heard you lost quite a few men."

"We did. Thousands. But so did they."

"Sorry, Colonel. I meant no offense."

"None taken. How'd you get here?"

Isaac rolled up the left sleeve on his shirt, an ugly scar making its appearance. "The Union butchers wanted to take my arm, but I wouldn't let 'em."

Isaac then pointed to his face.

"My fault. I refused to be captured."

The colonel smirked.

"But you were captured."

"I'm not dead yet, and I intend to take a few of those rebel bastards with me when I leave this place."

The colonel pointed to one of the men at his side.

"I want you to meet Major Hamilton."

Isaac and the major shook hands.

The colonel stepped closer to Isaac, speaking in a whisper.

"The Major thinks we've had enough of this rebel hospitality and would like to leave."

Isaac studied the major. The major stared back until Isaac smiled.

"Yes, sir," Isaac said.

The colonel leaned in once more, his voice barely audible.

"Say anything to anyone, and I'll kill you myself."

Lucas, his morning chores finished, sat on the front porch of the farmhouse.

He held the baby, Rebecca inside making coffee, genuinely enjoying his role as a surrogate father to little Isaac. It became habit for the trio to gather for coffee and often breakfast. George, usually absent, almost always left immediately after chores, to share the morning meal with his wife. Lucas, now bouncing the baby on his knee, prompted a laugh from the child and a look of approval from Rebecca.

"He likes you," said Rebecca, placing a cup of steaming hot coffee on the porch railing, a safe distance from the child.

"He's such a good baby, easy to love," he said.

Lucas searched Rebecca's face for a reaction. After all, he was more of a father to the child than the boy's natural father. He regularly fed the baby, changed him, played with the boy, and put him to bed. Lucas, now living in the barn because of the threat from Calhoun, relished the arrangement. The room and board cost nothing, and he enjoyed his proximity to the mother and her child. I am more than just the hired hand, thought Lucas. If it wasn't for him, the barn would have been a total loss. Indeed, after the fire, she insisted that he stop calling her Mrs. Wells, citing their insignificant age difference. Most importantly, several months passed since Isaac became a Confederate prisoner. He could be dead, and Rebecca must be thinking the same thoughts. Rebecca should move on, thought Lucas, and Lucas stood ready for the next step.

"I have a present for you, Rebecca."

"Lucas, there is no need for a present. I could not manage this place without you. You are present enough, and then some."

"Look, they're here."

Lucas pointed to the road. A slow-moving caravan of horses and wagons plus a dozen men turned into the drive.

"Are they coming here?" she asked.

"Yes, I did more than get supplies last week. I visited with your farmer friends at the general store. Seems like you made quite the impression. They're here to fix the barn."

Lucas, seeing the tears welling up in her eyes, placed the baby in his crib.

"Did I do the right thing?"

Rebecca rushed forward and threw her arms around the young man. His shirt absorbed the sounds of her sobs and the tears on her cheeks. After a while, she stepped back.

"I'm sorry, I shouldn't be carrying on so."

She kissed the boy, lightly on his cheek.

"Thank you, Lucas, thank you. You are a true friend."

Lucas reached for her shoulders, intending to kiss the woman, but Rebecca bowed, and he was reduced to a quick peck on her forehead.

"I would do anything for you, Rebecca."

Colonel Rose and Major Hamilton spoke in whispers so low that Isaac strained to hear their words. The men would tunnel their way to freedom.

Besides the colonel and the major, there would be thirteen men assigned to the tunnel. They would work in three shifts of five men each. Their tools would be pocket knives, clam shells, a piece of rope, and an old wooden spittoon. Their first task was to penetrate the brick fireplace behind the two stoves in the first-floor kitchen.

Once in the chimney, they would have access to the basement, better known as Rat Hell. The cellar, home to hundreds of rodents, also included four, currently unoccupied dungeons where the most dangerous of the inmates were occasionally held. It took the men two weeks of steady work to remove the bricks behind the kitchen stove. Each morning, the bricks were carefully returned to their original position so as to avoid detection.

Isaac's first foray into Rat Hell left him shocked and traumatized. The tunnel, barely two feet long and less than two feet in diameter, made it difficult to breathe much less maneuver in the damp hole. The rats, hundreds of them, squealed loudly when disturbed and regularly ran over Isaac's legs and back. The braver rodents ventured onto his neck and head, interested in the soft flesh of Isaac's earlobes. Each time Isaac brushed them away, they responded with a deafening chorus of squeals.

The five men on each shift took turns performing a variety of tasks. The first did digging and filled the spittoon with dirt. The second used the rope to pull the spittoon from the tunnel, the digger unable to move in any direction. The third man distributed the dirt underneath some straw in a pitch-dark corner of the basement. The fourth man waved a rubber sheet to force air into the tunnel, and the fifth man served as a lookout.

The inmates' ultimate objective, a large sewer pipe that connected the facility to the James River, lay dozens of yards away. After several weeks of round-the-clock digging, the men reached the sewer pipe. Captain Rose led Isaac's five-man team on that night, wanting to be the first man to break through. As he scraped at the last few inches of remaining soil, a steady flow of water muddied the ground on which the colonel was laying. As he removed more soil, more water flowed and rushed into the tunnel. Within minutes, Rose struggled to keep his head above the onslaught but was limited by the small diameter of the tunnel. He yelled for help; Isaac scrambled closer and pulled the officer to safety. The tunnel, now flooded, could not be used as an escape route.

In the weeks to come, the men made more attempts. The next tunnel also led to a sewer pipe but the tunnel collapsed, before the sewer line was reached. A third attempt to yet another pipe did not fail because of flood or collapse but, being too small, the line could not accommodate even the smallest prisoner. After the third failed attempt, Colonel Rose called a late-night meeting. The men openly grumbled, several resisting any further efforts to escape.

"We're wasting our time," said one man.

"It's too dangerous," said another.

"Time is all we have. And die here or die in the tunnel. Makes no difference to me," said Isaac.

Colonel Rose smiled and nodded in Isaac's direction. He turned to the rest of the diggers.

"Let's take a rest. The Major and I will look at our options, and we'll meet again in a week or so. Is that acceptable?"

The men nodded and murmured their approval, a number of them leaving the meeting for some badly needed rest.

Isaac crawled to his spot on the floor and fell asleep, exhausted from weeks of useless digging.

Chapter 30

Hope

Lucas and the farmer's group made quick work of the repairs to Rebecca's barn.

A home-cooked meal to thank the men disappeared as quickly as Rebecca's fire-scarred barn. With the last dish washed and put away, the hired hand enjoyed a moment alone with the lady of the house. Even baby Isaac, off to the village with Mrs. Lobdell, could not interrupt them. Lucas swallowed hard and took a deep breath.

"Rebecca, there is something I've been meaning to talk to you about."

Rebecca, her back to Lucas and busy folding a small mountain of baby clothes, compliments of an overzealous Mrs. Lobdell, showed no sign of hearing Lucas's nervous plea, folding the clothes, occasionally stopping to stare at the wall, and then returning to the laundry. He decided to repeat himself when she interrupted Lucas with a question of her own.

"Do you think Isaac is still alive?"

The question made the young man blush, Isaac's fate very much on Lucas's mind. The demise of Rebecca's husband, while tragic, simplified things. Lucas, free to court Rebecca, could pursue the woman with whom he was now in love. He hesitated, wondering if Rebecca noticed the flush of heat on his face and uncertain if he should voice his innermost thoughts.

"Well, I don't rightly know," he said.

Lucas, frustrated with himself, regretted his response, thinking it foolish.

"I am most fortunate to have you at my side," said Rebecca.

She turned, catching his nervous stare.

"How could I possibly manage without you. You're a very special young man."

He took a tentative step in her direction, thinking another warm embrace might be in the offing. But Rebecca turned back to her pile of clothes, grabbed one of the baby's outfits, and then threw it back on the pile.

"I'm exhausted, and I'm going to my room. Please extinguish the lamps on your way out."

Lucas studied his attractive employer as she walked down the hall and shut the bedroom door behind her. He frowned, huffing the flames out in each lamp, first in the parlor and then in the kitchen.

As he left the farmhouse, shutting the door with more force than usual, Lucas fixated on Rebecca, his thoughts not entirely innocent.

Rebecca floated into a deepening sleep, vaguely aware of the kitchen floorboards as they creaked. Her fuzzy mind, unable to sense the danger, urged her to sleep rather than run. She never heard the shoes as they approached her bedroom door and did not realize the presence of an intruder, until she could no longer breathe, her mouth now covered with a gloved hand. She woke from her sleepy stupor as the intruder pinned one of her arms to the bed. Her bewildered brain required a few seconds more to process the reality of a bedside assailant. She swung her loose arm at his masked head and sank her teeth deep into the glove. Her attacker, still trying to capture the loose arm, turned his head when she yanked the neckerchief from his face. Although still masked by the darkness, she could see the glare of his eyes and spit in their direction. She could smell the booze on his breath, the stink of his sweat. Her stepfather's bloodied and disfigured face made a brief appearance, but she did not submit. Rebecca screamed and resisted with a renewed fury. The monster's head growled at her.

"You stubborn bitch."

She recognized the gravelly voice and hissed her response through clenched teeth.

"Calhoun."

Now enraged, he released her arm and swung at Rebecca's face with his bony fist causing a loud crack followed by a soft moan and then–silence. She lay there, perfectly still, a limp doll of rags underneath his straddled legs. He paused just long enough to catch his breath, reached for the pillow, covered her face, and leaned hard.

Lucas rose from his bed of straw, used both hands to yank the hat over his head, and shoved his stockinged feet into his boots, not bothering to pull the pant legs over their tops. He stormed out of the barn, covering the distance to the farmhouse with his long strides and making no effort to soften the clunk of heels on the hardwood as he bound onto the porch. He banged on the front door, somewhere, a dog began to bark.

"Rebecca, wake up. It's high time we had a talk."

He heard a rustling noise from inside the house, but the door did not open. He banged again, abandoning any pretense of patience or politeness. Lucas hesitated, but only for a second, and then reached for the doorknob. The door flew open but it wasn't Rebecca on the other side, a strange man instead was swinging his fist toward Lucas's face. The farm boy veered back and then plunged forward, the two of them falling, and now rolling, on the kitchen floor. A glimmer of sharpened steel and stabbing pain in his left shoulder triggered the adrenalin in Lucas's body. Both men grabbed with both hands for the knife, each trying to control the weapon's wild swings. The boy, having the advantage of two muscular arms, slowly pushed the blade toward Calhoun's chest. Lucas forced the pointed steel to within an inch of the man's shirt, now covered with the farm boy's blood. For a brief moment, there was no motion, no heavy breathing, not even a painful grunt–just silence, deadly silence. Lucas took a deep breath, squeezed his eyes shut, and pushed with all of his weight. Calhoun groaned and then exhaled, long, and hard. Suddenly, it was quiet, eerily still, until Lucas slid from his perch on the dead man's torso and struggled to light a nearby lamp with hands that shook like a leaf in the wind.

"Rebecca, can you hear me? Rebecca, talk to me please."

Rebecca struggled to focus on the face that called her name. She smiled and then groaned from the self-inflicted pain. She recognized Lucas and consciously opened her mouth but quickly surrendered to the excruciating agony of a broken jaw. She mumbled through bruised and lacerated lips but still, he did not understand.

"Are you all right?"

Rebecca's eyes burned with tears of pain; she moved her head from side to side.

"That's all right. I'll do the talking. You've been out cold for a while. George got here a little while after sun up. He went to fetch the doc and Sheriff Bromley."

Rebecca blinked her approval. Lucas, contemplating all that had taken place, took a few sharp breaths. He turned to her, his lips quivering, his hands jerking up to cover his face. In a muffled voice, he confessed to his murderous act.

"That man that attacked you, he pulled a knife on me. I killed him, Rebecca. I killed him."

She pulled him close, careful to keep her hand between his head and her jaw. The young man sobbed into her nightdress, soaking the cotton with his tears.

Rebecca patted him on the back, genuinely concerned for his health and well-being.

She gave no thought to the demons of her past.

Isaac, after a week of rest, prepared to dig another tunnel.

Colonel Rose and Major Hamilton presented the details of their fourth attempt to escape Libby Prison. The whispered plan, to dig in the direction of a lot adjacent to the prison's east wall, specified that the tunnel should go under a fence that surrounded a small tobacco shed. From there the escapees could swim across the James River and from that point, it would be every man for himself.

No one spent more time in Rat Hell than Isaac Wells. Obsessed with the project, he rarely slept for more than a few hours at a time and constantly monitored the men's progress. Isaac rotated from the tunnel to the spittoon to the rubber sheet and then to guard duty. He often took double shifts. On a rare day of rest, the colonel approached.

"You get to bring a friend with you when we leave this place."

"I don't have any friends," said Isaac.

"You've been angry since the day you arrived. What's eating at you, Boy?"

Isaac, sitting cross-legged on the floor, used the dull nub of his case-knife to remove dirt from underneath his fingernails. He scraped a few more nails clean, stopped and glared at the colonel.

"I've been digging my share and then some. What do you want from me?"

The colonel stared out the barred window and bit his lip. He turned to Isaac.

"Forget I asked."

"I will."

"Tonight, we have to get our bearings," said the colonel.

"How?" Isaac asked.

"When we get about ten feet out, we'll need a small hole to the surface. Shove this through the hole; it'll be our marker."

The colonel dropped an old shoe in Isaac's lap.

"We check tomorrow, at sunup. If the shoe is in the right place, we're headed in the right direction."

"I'll do it tonight." Isaac returned to his dirty nails.

"Thank you, Lieutenant."

As the colonel walked away, Isaac paused and looked up. No one ever addressed him as a lieutenant before.

Isaac shook a rat off his arm as he poked and scraped at the ceiling of the tunnel. The nosy rodent landed on a dozen more rats, and they all squealed in protest. Isaac, worried that the sentries would hear the high-pitched racket, refused to shoo the animals away, suffering bites as a result. He poked at the dirt ceiling in his tunnel long enough to cover his hair with dirt. Although his eyes, half blinded from the falling debris, could not see the hole, a blast of cold air on his face told Isaac that he reached the surface. He made the hole just large enough to shove the old shoe into the opening and took a moment to catch his breath. Then he whispered loudly to the inmate with the rope.

"Let's go."

The men exited the tunnel, replaced the bricks behind the stove, and reported back to the colonel.

"We'll check the window first thing tomorrow morning," said the colonel.

He focused on Isaac.

"Good work, Wells."

Isaac didn't hear the compliment. He had fallen asleep.

Chapter 31

Freedom

"It's broken."

Doc McLean delivered the unsurprising news to Rebecca about her jaw. He proposed to immobilize her lower jaw leaving just enough space for her to consume liquids. Although none of her teeth were broken, he estimated that the fracture needed weeks to heal. As Rebecca submitted to the doctor's ministrations, Sheriff Bromley appeared at her bedroom door.

"Your hired hand is in bad shape."

Rebecca furrowed her eyebrows, questioning the sheriff with her face.

"He did nothing wrong. He was forced to defend himself. George is with him now, drinking some of your whiskey."

Rebecca smiled and then frowned. She motioned to the sheriff for a pencil and some paper. After a few minutes, he returned, and Rebecca scribbled a series of notes. She wrote instructions for the hired hands, a note to Mrs. Lobdell to keep the baby at her place, and a request for someone, anyone, to check the post office. The young woman, desperate for word from her imprisoned husband, pointed out that portion of her note, for emphasis.

Rebecca stopped writing when her neighbor, Mrs. Burns, walked into the bedchamber. She shooed all of Rebecca's visitors from the bedroom, including Doc McLean, who surveyed with satisfaction, the unsightly contraption that would keep Rebecca's lower jaw immobilized.

"Don't you worry about a thing, Miss Rebecca. I'll be staying here until you get better. Don't you worry about a thing."

The neighbor lady busied herself straightening the bedchamber and retrieving extra pillows for her patient. She then disappeared into the kitchen, announcing on her way out of the bedroom, a breakfast of chicken broth and coffee.

Rebecca closed her eyes, relieved and exhausted.

Progress on the tunnel came in fits and spurts, depending on the hardness of the Virginia soil. Colonel Rose's fourth attempt measured in excess of fifty feet.

Isaac, his case-knife now a worn stub of dull metal, also broke several of the palm-sized clamshells, in his hurry to reach the tobacco shed. The colonel's old shoe confirmed that the men were headed in the correct direction. And while Rose could only eyeball the men's progress, he convinced himself that the tunnel now reached within the confines of the small tobacco shed. He spoke to the team of diggers but focused on Isaac.

"I think it's time we shoved a head through the top of our tunnel."

Isaac stabbed the floor with his knife and fixated on the colonel.

"We can do it tonight."

"Unless there's a problem, be prepared to move tomorrow, after dark," said the colonel to the rest of his men. An audible wave of murmuring approvals and whispered exaltations spread through the assembled group. The colonel reminded his men of the need for secrecy, but by day's end, the entire prison knew of the pending escape.

Rose was right behind Isaac as the enlisted-man-turned-lieutenant, did the honors, bringing another shower of dirt onto his head and face. Eventually, the hole, now blowing a cool, refreshing breeze into the tunnel, grew wide enough for Isaac's head. He looked at the Colonel, took a deep breath, and pushed his head through the gaping hole. When Isaac opened his eyes, he saw nothing but inky darkness. After a moment, his eyes adjusted and Isaac could see the slight glow of a starlit evening seeping through the cracks in a loose-fitting door. The colonel, forced to wait a moment longer as Isaac savored the clean, fresh air, tugged on Isaac's pant leg.

"What do you see? Talk to me, Boy."

Isaac collapsed to a crawling position.

"We're in the shed, Colonel. Dead center."

He could feel the colonel's hand squeeze the calf on his leg.

"You done good, Lieutenant. You done good."

Isaac did not acknowledge the officer's praise, busy, instead, trying to cover the hole with some dirt and a small piece of plastic sheet.

It was three in the morning on February 9.

"I know you can't speak, but I have something to say."

Rebecca, several weeks into her recovery, moved about the kitchen, performing light chores in the farmhouse. Lucas sat at the table, watching his employer.

"Do you know why I came back to the house that night?"

Rebecca stopped what she was doing and moved to the table, her tea waiting for her. He looked away, hesitated for a moment, and then jerked his head in her direction. He didn't blink.

"I love you, Miss Rebecca. I love you. There I said it."

The boy's eyes were glassy, his voice shook. Rebecca's cup rattled in its saucer, her freehand rose to cover a smothered gasp, grateful for her temporary disability, uncertain as to how she should respond.

"I'm sorry, Rebecca, I'm sorry. But I had to tell you."

Rebecca reached for her paper and pencil. Her eyes closed and she waited, hoping the right words would flow from her pencil.

Lucas stared at the upside-down words. He reached for the hand that was writing and shook his head.

"Stop."

Rebecca pushed his hand away and returned to her note. Without warning, she dropped the pencil on the table, as if it burned her hand. Rebecca flipped the paper right side up and pushed it in his direction, pointing to a single word. She stared at him, waiting for a response. Lucas bowed his head and muttered what she now knew.

"I can't read, Miss Rebecca."

"Rebecca thought for a moment and started to draw. It was a large heart. But then, she drew an even larger "x" through the heart. She pushed it towards Lucas and reached for his hand. The illiterate, young man recoiled, brushed the paper to the floor with the back of his hand, and jumped out of his chair. Rebecca blinked and leaned back, afraid of what he might do next.

Lucas stormed out of the kitchen, slamming the door behind him.

Colonel Rose decreed that teams of thirty men each, spaced one hour apart, would enter the tunnel.

Non-diggers received detailed briefings on what to expect, including lots of rats and a very narrow escape route, the men encouraged to keep one arm forward and the other arm pinned to their back, to facilitate movement. Although several men prepared for the long crawl and cold swim by exercising in advance, most arrived at the entrance to the tunnel, malnourished, poorly clothed, and suffering from a variety of ailments.

Isaac watched the first group of thirty, led by Colonel Rose, as they disappeared into the basement. The second group led by Major Hamilton included Isaac. Rose announced his intention to reach Williamsburg, some fifty miles away. Hamilton, inclined to do the same, simply shrugged when Isaac announced his plan, to reach the Pamunkey River and follow it back to Hanover.

After the first and second groups disappeared from their third-floor lair, chaos and confusion spread like wildfire through the prison. There was pushing, shoving, some yelling, and plenty of negotiations amongst prisoners who bartered for a place in the line; the scuffle enveloped the entire third floor. Isaac, worried that the guards would be alerted, welcomed his rat friends, who by comparison made less noise. Once in the shed, he dusted himself off, pulled his collar up, and opened the door as slowly as he could. Isaac, careful not to alarm the nearby sentry, noted that the guard stood near a fire barrel, too busy warming himself to notice the tobacco shed. Isaac tried not to splash as he waded into the James River–the ice-cold water causing him to inhale sharply and tremble with violence he had never experienced. As he swam, almost silently, to the other side, he heard a desperate whisper.

"Help me, help me please."

Isaac could see nothing in the darkness and quickened his pace when the pleading voice splashed and the gurgling noise got louder. Before he reached the other side, the silence told Isaac that his fellow inmate, so close to freedom, had been captured by the James River. Isaac calculated that the thirty-mile trip to the Pamunkey River and Union camps, although more difficult, remained the shortest route to safety. After walking less than an hour, Isaac saw only barren tobacco fields and the occasional wooded area. He used the North Star, often blocked by clouds, to verify that he was headed in a northerly direction.

Voices in the dark and the slight smell of smoke brought him to a sudden halt. Motionless and afraid, he strained to hear the voices, desperate to know if enemy soldiers were nearby. The unmistakable vernacular of a black man was like music to Isaac's ears as he ventured closer to the voice. He approached the campsite with caution, however, making no noise as he did so. Four men and one woman, with a small fire in their midst, roasted what appeared to be the carcass of a squirrel. Their dinner, tended to by the woman, was being observed by the men, who sat perched on a nearby tree, long ago destroyed by water and rot. Isaac stepped out from behind a large bush and showed himself, his hands in the air, but the almost useless case-knife hidden from view in the waistband of his pants. The men leapt to their feet, one of them brandishing what appeared to be a crudely fashioned walking stick. The woman froze in place.

"I'm a Union soldier. I mean no harm."

"Is you alone?" asked the man with the stick.

"Yes, sir."

The inquiry was followed by silence, the white man carefully surveying his reluctant hosts; the black men, and their female companion, studying the white man in blue.

"I was at Libby Prison. Escaped last night."

The inky darkness was slowly transforming itself into a faint light, announcing the morning sun that would soon bring some desperately needed heat. But still, no one moved.

"Weeze not runaways, if that's what you thinkin'," said the stick man.

"I am," said Isaac, making his first attempt at humor in months.

The woman smiled.

"You like squirrel?"

"Yes, ma'am."

The black man tossed his wooden weapon on the ground and motioned the others to sit. He turned to Isaac.

"Pull up a log."

Chapter 32

News

"I'm being fired."

Lucas, in the barn finishing his morning chores, turned and greeted Rebecca with his back. The two avoided each other for weeks, giving Rebecca the time she needed to master a garbled version of the English language.

"No, you are not being fired. I made some coffee. Will you join me in the kitchen, please?"

He nodded and followed his boss to the farmhouse, watching her closely. The awful contraption now gone, Rebecca exhibited no symptoms from the awful attack which almost killed her, several months ago.

They both stomped the snow and muck off their feet as they entered the kitchen, neither of them wishing to soil the spotless room. Lucas, with his hat in hand, remained on the braided rug next to the door.

"There is no need to stand, Lucas."

Rebecca poured the coffee, occasionally glancing at the young man she had spurned, and feeling guilty for having done so. Despite the now awkward nature of their relationship, Rebecca appreciated Lucas, the young man now an excellent farmhand thanks to the instruction he received from George. She thought the boy ready for bigger and better things.

"I have decided to buy old man Fulton's place," she announced.

Lucas pushed his coffee to the center of the table, untouched. He refused to make eye contact with Rebecca, focusing instead on the blowing snow rushing past the kitchen window.

"I don't see how this concerns me," said Lucas.

"I want you to manage the new farm."

The boy's head snapped to attention.

"I don't understand."

Rebecca smiled and slowly pushed the exiled coffee cup back to his side of the table.

"Fulton's farmhouse is small, but I'm sure you'll find it acceptable. You must promise to come and visit. Baby Isaac would miss you terribly."

Lucas, pulling at his hair and grinning widely, blushed and then reached for his coffee.

"Thank you, Rebecca, I mean, Mrs. Wells. Thank you."

Rebecca also announced that Lucas needed to hire a helper and that an increase in the boy's pay should be expected. His new job included the need to train and supervise the new man. After a few moments, the tension between them disappeared, and they talked at length about Rebecca's new investment, their plans for spring, and the need for a new hired hand at the Wells' family farm. When each ran out of things to say, Rebecca rose to her feet, Lucas quickly followed.

"Lucas, I want you to be happy."

"I'm not an educated man, Miss Rebecca, but I know a good woman when I see one. You're good people, and I am much obliged."

Lucas retrieved his hat from the table and took a few halting steps toward the door. He turned, and the two stared at each other in an awkward moment of silence. Rebecca took a few steps in his direction.

"I wish to embrace my good friend. Is that acceptable to you?" she asked.

Lucas rushed to Rebecca, threw his arms around her and delivered a bear hug that lifted her off the floor.

"Hugs are always acceptable," he shouted.

"Private Isaac Wells, with the 118th from New York."

Isaac, barely able to stand, required days to reach Hanover and stopped the first bluecoat he saw. Too weak to stand for long periods of time and famished, two soldiers ushered him to the courthouse and brought food and water.

The courthouse, temporary headquarters for many of the Union troops in that area of the Pamunkey River, housed several officers, all of them eager to hear of Isaac's daring escape. The details of his thirty-mile journey and Isaac's description of the horrible conditions at Libby Prison mesmerized his audience. The men openly expressed their horror but also their admiration for the dozens of soldiers who managed to escape.

"If we waited for Lincoln to get off his ass, I'd still be there," said Isaac, his stay in prison only fueling his animosity toward the president.

Unfortunately, no one at the courthouse seemed to know the whereabouts of the 118th. The colonel ordered Isaac to take the next train to Washington and report to the War Department.

"They'll take forever, and you could use the rest, Wells," said the colonel.

The boy, now freshly provisioned and with the proper uniform, slept for most of the ride to his nation's capital. Familiar with the city, Isaac reported to the war department, in search of his newest assignment. He discovered that the military bureaucracy had no agreed-upon procedure to deal with recruits that had escaped their Confederate captors. It did not happen very often. News of the escape from Libby spread through Washington like a brushfire, Isaac learning from fellow soldiers that while dozens of his fellow inmates escaped, roughly half were recaptured. The remainder, scattered all over Virginia, showed up in a variety of locations but only Isaac reappeared in Washington.

"What are my orders? Where is my regiment?" he asked.

He questioned a clerk at the war department who seemed as confused as the soldier.

"That's up to the colonel, but he's not here today."

"Where do I stay?"

"I can't answer that, Private."

Isaac shook his head in disgust and walked the streets of Washington, until he recognized the hospital where he wrote letters for the soldiers and met President Lincoln. If he met the president today, thought Isaac, the meeting would not be nearly as pleasant. He mentally tallied the list of complaints, including lousy food, if there was food at all, paydays that never arrived on time, prisoners of war effectively abandoned, and no apparent end in sight to this God-awful war. It seemed Lincoln had lost his way and Isaac, beyond disappointed, nursed a deep-seated hatred for the man.

As he entered the hospital, the long-ago sights, sounds, and smells came rushing back. But a different Isaac Wells walked through the entrance today, this one no longer interested in helping his fellow soldier and no longer eager to serve his country. "Wells, isn't it?"

One orderly recognized the boy from Keeseville.

"Guilty."

"You don't look any better than the last time you were here," said the orderly.

Isaac, too tired to complain about the insult, refused to acknowledge his former colleague.

"I need a place to stay. The war department doesn't know what to do with me. I escaped from a Confederate prison, and I don't know where to find my regiment."

"Are you one of those guys who escaped from Libby Prison?"

"One of the lucky ones."

"Everyone is talking about it. The biggest escape ever. Tell me about it, please?"

"First, a place to sleep and then we'll talk."

"Yes, sir," said the orderly, happy to oblige one man who made history.

"You're lucky."

The colonel at the war department explained to Isaac that the 118th, now on its way to White House, Virginia, suffered unimaginable casualties at Proctor's Creek and Drury's Bluff. Two hundred men were killed, wounded or missing in action.

"You can join them at White House."

"I would like to have been there," Isaac replied.

"No, Private Wells, you would not have liked it."

Another train ride and the warrior returned to what remained of his regiment. The 118th had changed–the men were solemn, many of them depressed, and most of them, missed their homes. Isaac's arrival seemed to be a welcome respite from the horrors of battle, a glimmer of hope to those who had little, if any hope at all. When word spread that Private Wells was one of the lucky escapees from Libby Prison, the Keeseville boy became a camp-wide distraction. Isaac, reluctant and openly uncooperative with his colleagues, withstood constant questions about the prison and the escape. They pressed for details but offered a few tidbits of information that Isaac had not yet heard. Several escapees drowned in the James River. Colonel Rose was recaptured, and no, there were no plans for Union troops to raid the prison, despite its horrible conditions. Isaac, still angry and bitter about his stay at the prison, and the conduct of the war itself, experienced a twinge of guilt when he heard about Colonel Rose.

Many of the lads plied Isaac with rations, foodstuffs from home, and a variety of gifts, in return for some time with the local celebrity. Isaac preferred to keep to himself and became adamant about his solitude.

"Here, I thought you might like these."

The soldier, whose face was familiar but not his name, tossed some newspapers on Isaac's cot.

"No thanks."

Isaac's unwanted visitor was undeterred.

"I'm from Port Kent. These are local papers. My mother sent them to me with some cornbread, but I ate the cornbread."

The visitor smiled, Isaac reached for the papers.

"You got a name?"

"Alonzo Wilson."

"What do you want to know?"

Isaac answered most of Wilson's queries but took umbrage when Wilson pointed out that Libby was for officers only.

"My lieutenant smuggled me in."

Isaac paused for a moment, staring at his shoes.

"Didn't do him much good, though, he's dead."

Wilson said nothing, sensing he had overstayed his unwelcome.

"You finished?" Isaac asked.

"Yes sir, thank you, sir. Enjoy the papers."

Isaac scanned the newsprint, two issues of the *Essex County Republican* and one issue of the Plattsburgh paper, all of them, weeks old. The Plattsburgh paper offered nothing of interest, but a headline in the *Essex County Republican* caught his attention.

'Intruder Stabbed with His Own Knife'

Isaac's eyes grew into small saucers as he read the details. At one point, he looked around, wanting no one in the vicinity to see what he saw. The names were screaming at him; *'Wells' family farm, Lucas Alcott, Rebecca Wells.*

Isaac, not familiar with the dead man, focused again and again, on one line in the story.

'Calhoun attacked Wells in the middle of the night, but Alcott came to her rescue.'

His initial reaction–that Rebecca had survived the ordeal–quickly turned to curiosity. Within minutes, he asked himself the question that burned in his brain. Why was Lucas Alcott at his farmhouse at that time of the evening? Isaac re-read the entire article. He threw the paper across the room, paced the floor, returned to his cot, retrieved the paper, and read it again. The words had not changed, Lucas Alcott, the hero.

Isaac Wells felt like a gullible fool.

Chapter 33

Shattered

Rebecca avoided thoughts of her missing husband by devoting most of her days and many of her evenings tending to the demands of two operating farms and a sixteen-month-old toddler.

She wisely surrounded herself with able people like George, Lucas and her mother, becoming accustomed to taking charge of matters large and small, domestic and otherwise. As she left the post office in Keeseville, another wasted trip in search of word from her warrior husband, Rebecca spied a familiar face.

"Good afternoon, Mr. Putnam."

The schoolmaster, old enough to be Rebecca's father, embraced the young woman.

"Any word from our friend?"

Rebecca, her eyes downcast and bravely blinking back the tears, did not have to respond. Putnam reacted with words of encouragement.

"You have become the talk of the town, Mrs. Wells. Surviving that dreadful attack, raising a child, and running not one but two farms, and with no husband at your side. I, for one, am most impressed."

Rebecca wiped her tears with a small white handkerchief and smiled her appreciation.

"Thank you, Mr. Putnam. You are most kind and a marvelously effective elixir for my soul."

Putnam bowed his head and smiled.

"The pleasure is all mine, Mrs. Wells."

"Mr. Putnam, please forgive me if I am being forward. But I am spending the evening in town and will be by myself. Would you care to join me for dinner? As my guest, of course."

Putnam's face lit up, and this time he bowed from the waist.

"It would be my distinct pleasure to dine with you, Mrs. Wells."

Later that evening, the older gentleman and the young lady enjoyed a meal at the Ausable House dining room. Rebecca related news of the great escape from Libby Prison.

"The rebels took Isaac prisoner, not far from there. Perhaps he escaped with the rest of those men."

Mr. Putnam returned his cup of tea to its saucer, wiped his mouth with the white cloth napkin, and peered over his wire-rim glasses, no longer smiling.

"Mrs. Wells, I hesitate to say anything, since our evening together has been so pleasant."

"Please, Mr. Putnam, there is nothing you can do or say that will discourage me. I will always hope and pray for the safe return of my dear Isaac."

"I am confidently informed that Libby Prison is for the incarceration of officers only."

Rebecca reached for her water, the blood draining from her face, her hands trembling as she brought the glass to her lips. She forced herself to swallow and used the distraction to calm her nerves.

"Are you certain, Mr. Putnam?"

Putnam bit his lower lip and stared at the uneaten vegetables on his plate.

"Where would they have taken him?" she asked.

"There are a number of possibilities, I'm afraid."

"Please, not Andersonville, please."

Mr. Putnam folded his napkin, changed his mind, and then crumpled it, slamming the embroidered snowball onto the plate.

He said nothing. He didn't have to.

"I have come here to request a furlough."

Isaac, standing in front of the captain's oversized desk, realized that hundreds of people had come to the courthouse in Hanover, to plead their case. Isaac assumed his wish would be granted.

"I know you're some sort of hero in these parts, Private Wells, but there is a chain of command for these sorts of things," said the captain.

"I've been to the sergeant, the corporal, the lieutenant, and just about everybody else in this godforsaken place, and they all sent me to you."

"Why do you have to go home?"

"It's personal."

"That's not good enough, Private."

"My wife was almost killed by an intruder."

Isaac handed his newspaper to the captain, calculating that his commanding officer would not understand what Isaac had read. The captain studied the newspaper, looked twice at the date, and tossed the paper onto his desk.

"This paper is more than a month old. Has your wife recovered?"

"Yes, sir, but. . ."

"Is she alone?"

"Well, her mother lives in the village but. . ."

"You're needed here, Wells. We march to Cold Harbor, tomorrow."

"But Captain, you don't understand."

"Your request for a furlough is denied. Dismissed."

Isaac saluted, turned on one foot, and returned to his tent. He shoved a few things into his haversack, checked his sidearm to verify that it was fully loaded, and jogged to where the horses were tied.

"You're the guy who escaped from Libby prison."

Isaac rolled his eyes and shook his head, but he was on a mission and couldn't be bothered with the inquiring sentry.

"That's correct, Private, and if you don't mind, I'll be borrowing this horse for a bit."

Isaac grabbed a saddle and started toward one of the horses.

"Sorry, sir, no one's allowed to take a horse without the captain's permission."

Isaac continued, pulling the cinch and reaching for a bridle.

"I just left the captain."

"I need to see his orders, sir."

Isaac ignored the private's request and reached for the rope that tethered the animal to its tie line. Without warning, the sentry fired his rifle sending a Minié ball within earshot of Isaac's head. Isaac froze in place, his back to the guard.

"You wouldn't shoot a war hero in the back, would you, Private?"

"I'm sorry, sir, I have my orders. If I let you ride out of here on one of those horses, they'll hang me for sure. Please, sir, don't make me do it."

Isaac turned, the bridle still in his hand, and for a brief moment, he studied the rifle barrel now pointed at his chest. The horses fidgeted, despite their familiarity with the noise of weaponry. Several men came running, including the sergeant.

"Are you looking to scare off the horses, Private?"

The sentry focused on Isaac and then stared at the sergeant.

"No, sir."

The sergeant studied the saddled horse and noted the bridle in Isaac's hand.

"Private Wells, let's go for a walk."

Isaac refused to budge.

"Now!"

Isaac followed the sergeant into the deep woods.

Rebecca hosted Sunday dinner for her family and the hired hands.

Her mother, George, Lucas, the new men, and Mrs. Burns, along with baby Isaac, now a little more than two years old, ate their fill and enjoyed the afterglow of a fine meal. The men, in the parlor, talked farm animals and speculated whether or not the corn should be planted early, in this unseasonably warm year. The ladies cleaned up in the kitchen as they took turns chasing baby Isaac, in a constant effort to keep him out of trouble.

When darkness threatened, Mrs. Lobdell, announced that she would put little Isaac to bed and coaxed the boy to follow her, using his favorite blanket as a bribe. She returned to the kitchen a short while later and joined her daughter and Mrs. Burns for a relaxing cup of tea at the kitchen table.

"I wish I had that boy's energy," Mrs. Lobdell marveled.

The ladies chatted a bit longer about the boy, his absent father, and the endless war, Mrs. Lobdell, the first to surrender to her fatigue.

"Please forgive me, ladies. I'm tired, and it's time for me to get some rest."

As she rose from the chair, retrieving her empty teacup, Mrs. Lobdell hesitated. She turned away from her companions but halted in mid-step, the dishes now trembling in her hands. She reached to silence the china, but the cup and saucer crashed to the floor and splintered into pieces. Rebecca jumped to her feet, Mrs. Burns after her, and they caught the woman as she sank, first to her knees and then to a crumpled heap on the floor. The men, alerted by the noise, carried Mrs. Lobdell into the parlor laying her on the sofa. Rebecca rushed after her, Mrs. Burns decided on a glass of cold water. The sick woman's eyes were unfocused, her eyelids fluttering like the wings of a tiny bird on its maiden voyage.

"Momma, Momma, talk to me."

Rebecca's plea went unacknowledged, Mrs. Burns returned with the water.

"Drink this; you'll feel better," she said.

Mrs. Burns withdrew her offer when she saw the sick woman's blank stare. Rebecca leaned forward, grabbing her mother by the shoulders and shaking her lifeless form.

"Momma, Momma, talk to me. Talk to me, Momma."

Lucas and George, one on either side of their boss, tugged Rebecca to her feet.

"No. No. Please, Lord, no."

Mrs. Burns sobbed, the two newly-minted hired hands turned away. Lucas pulled Rebecca close, George covered the body with a nearby afghan.

They carried and pulled Rebecca to her father-in-law's rocking chair, her tears falling like rain, but not a sound from her lips.

The punishment for going AWOL is prison, if you're lucky, death by hanging if you're not."

The sergeant explained to Isaac the ramifications of the farm boy's decision to abandon his post.

"I have nothing to live for, Sergeant. Everything I ever wanted, everything I ever had, is gone.

"You got a wife, don't you?"

"No, I don't think I do."

"You get a letter from home?"

"No, I read it in a newspaper. It's a long story, Sarge, and I don't wanna talk about it."

"Come with me, Wells. I'll buy you a drink."

The two retreated to the sergeant's tent and emptied a bottle filled with cheap whiskey. The sergeant made sure that Isaac got more than his fair share. After the whiskey disappeared, Isaac, unable to walk, much less ride, was returned to his tent by the sergeant. He dumped the boy into the cot and pulled his legs off the ground.

"Enjoy your rest, Wells. Tomorrow, we go to war."

Although the 118th, scheduled to march at eight in the morning, delayed its departure until that evening, Isaac, nursing an incapacitating hangover, used the extra time to recover and prepare. The all-night march to Cold Harbor left the men, hot, dust-covered, and fatigued. The regiment, at half their usual strength, joined thousands of soldiers on arrival. To Isaac, it seemed like the entire Army of the Potomac floated up the Pamunkey River. General Burnham led the brigade and Major General Brooks led their division.

For a short while, the troops mingled, swapped war stories, and generally bolstered each other's morale. But soon the order came to advance into position and move within range of the enemy's guns. Isaac enjoyed a terrifying view of the Union Army's objective.

The enemy's front line, 1,400 yards away, included a line of pickets, some 300 yards closer to the Union troops. The open space between the two armies, well-guarded by enemy artillery, offered no shelter from Confederate fire. On either side of the battlefield, small wooded areas served as a possible safe haven for the wounded and less courageous.

The order to charge sounded at six that evening. The rebel picket fell quickly, Union troops gathering up more than 250 prisoners. The mainline of rebel defenses proved more difficult, a blistering fusillade of Minié balls and artillery shells, decimating the Blue line that rushed forward into the field. Hundreds of men fell, were killed or wounded, and the lucky ones, including Isaac, rushed for cover in the nearby forest. Isaac resisted a temptation to charge the enemy lines. He calculated that his chances of killing a few rebs before they killed him, as minimal. The boy no longer possessed a desire to live, but he wanted to do significant damage before he exited this never-ending war. Isaac sat with his back to the enemy, a large tree absorbing the hail of bullets and occasionally shedding a small branch in protest of the rebel assault. As darkness wrapped itself around the field of battle, silence smothered most of the fire-breathing weaponry on both sides. He settled in for the night, munching on hardtack and chasing the rock-hard substance down his throat with an occasional swig of warm water from his canteen. Using the tree as his pillow, and napping when able, Isaac woke in time to watch as the sun's rays showered the forest with beams of light. He turned to catch a glimpse of the battlefield and drew a sharp breath; his shock and horror were overwhelming. Hundreds of dust-covered bodies cluttered the field, many of them absent limbs, some cut in two, a few, without their heads. A pall of smoke, trapped by the Virginia heat and humidity, hovered close to the ground, Mother Nature's shroud until the dead could be buried. Some of the bodies moved, a few moaned, but no one dared to rescue their fallen comrades, less they, too, fall victim to the enemy's fire.

The men in blue, ordered to dig trenches, concluded that neither side would be advancing or retreating anytime soon. Although under constant fire, Isaac attacked the forest floor with a vengeance, his bayonet serving as a makeshift pickaxe, his hands, as shovels. His portion of the trench, now close to perfection, featured a protective berm for additional cover. Unfortunately, he received no reward for such fine work, instead he heard a series of bugle calls which signaled the order to charge. Isaac, disappointed that the unseen enemy would escape his wrath, reconciled himself to death on the battlefield, his mind numb, after months of depression, frustration, and anger.

When the final charge sounded, Isaac screamed at the top of his lungs, pointed his rifle, and ran toward the enemy. He didn't get far. A hammer blow to his left shin bone brought the boy to his knees and then to his side. He crawled on his belly and rolled into the safety of his own trench, panting and crouching low because the zip-zip of Minié balls surrounded his head. The wounded soldier pulled the growing red stain on his pant leg, to just below the knee. He groaned in pain as the unrecognizable mass of blood, bone, and tissue came into view.

Isaac's lower leg was shattered.

Chapter 34

Survival

Isaac's natural instinct to survive overwhelmed his death wish.

He fashioned a crude tourniquet with his neckerchief and contemplated his next move. If he abandoned his trench, there would be a withering hail of Minié balls and artillery shells. If he remained where he was, he would bleed to death.

Isaac stole a fleeting glance at the scene behind him. The series of earthen berms told him that his escape to the rear would be punctuated with hills and holes, danger and safety. Once again, the fatalist in Isaac took charge. He struggled to the top of his trench, and crawled on his belly at a furious pace, to the next trench, rolling onto a fellow soldier. But Isaac's trench mate did not complain, the upper portion of the man's head had been removed with the surgical precision of a well-placed bullet.

Isaac looked to the rear, once again. Some trenches, guarded by bodies stacked to absorb enemy fire, served as a shield for the occupants but created an obstacle for Isaac. Again, he abandoned the safety of one trench for the safety of another, dragging his useless limb behind him and screaming in pain as he did so. He scrambled over the dead sentries, some falling into their trench with Isaac as if they too were searching for cover. Isaac, exhausted to the point of collapse, reached the relative safety of those Union troops held in reserve.

Using his rifle as a crutch, he dared to walk the rest of the way to the camp hospital. Two soldiers with an empty litter rushed to

Isaac's side as he fell to his knees. Isaac didn't have to say anything, but he did.

"Help."

"Has the bleeding stopped?"

The voice belonged to a fat, bearded man, spectacles perched low on his nose, and stuffed into a blood-soaked apron. He was talking to a young soldier, ashen white and visibly unhappy with his current assignment as an orderly in the camp hospital. The orderly was examining a nearby patient.

Isaac stared upward, the dirty gray sky punctured with poles and ropes, telling him that he was lying on a cot in a large tent, the camp hospital. His sluggish return to full consciousness, serenaded by the moans and groans of wounded soldiers, brought with it the painful memory of his shattered leg. He lifted his head off the bed and noticed the small tent in the sheet, created by his right foot. The left side of the sheet lay flat. He hesitated, wet his lips, and then pulled the sheet toward his knees, exposing an unmolested right foot. He tugged some more, strained for a better view, but still no left foot. Drowning in panic, Isaac yanked the sheet to his waist and propped himself up on one elbow.

Where his lower leg used to be, he saw only sheet. A bloody bandage encased his knee, making it appear like an oversized piece of sausage.

"No, No, No."

He threw the sheet to the ground, pulled at his hair with both hands and screamed some more.

"What did you do? You're butchers, all of you. You hear me? Butchers."

The orderly and the old surgeon rushed to Isaac's side.

"Be still, or you'll bleed to death."

"I don't care. I'd rather be dead. Why didn't you just let me die? Oh God, please let me die."

"Drink this."

The orderly put Isaac into a headlock, the surgeon pinched the boy's nose and waited. When Isaac gasped for air, the old man poured a shot glass of liquid into the hole. Isaac continued to thrash and struggle but within moments, grew quiet.

His eyelids fluttered, and the tent went dark.

Isaac refused to eat or drink.

It had been days since the amputation and, despite pronouncements from the surgeon that Isaac's leg healed well, the boy remained angry, bitter, and suicidal. At one point, he managed to find a sidearm. But for the fact that it misfired, Isaac might have been granted his death wish.

"They can fit you with a wooden leg."

The surgeon, in a rare moment of no emergencies, stood over Isaac's cot with a half-empty bottle of whiskey in his hand.

"Care for a drink?"

Isaac swung hard with the back of his right hand, sending the bottle flying. The surgeon stepped back, using his open palms as a chest-high shield from his patient's anger.

"Listen to me, Boy. I didn't shoot your leg off. The rebels did that. I saved your life."

"You ruined my life. I wish I was dead."

"Well, you're not. And the way I figure it, you got two choices, a fake leg or loaded pistol."

"They took my gun."

"You're leaving for Washington tomorrow. Some fellow named Palmer invented a wood and leather contraption. They say it works the same as a leg. The hospital will see that you're fitted right and proper."

"I don't want a fake leg."

"It'll help you walk."

"I don't wanna walk."

"You're gonna have to walk."

"Why?"

"You're going home."

"He's alive."

Lucas came running into the farmhouse with a copy of the local newspaper.

"Mr. Putnam gave this to me. It says that Isaac Wells is alive."

Rebecca grabbed the newsprint from Lucas's hands and spread it on the kitchen table. She scanned the print, turned the page, and studied the paper some more. Suddenly, she pointed.

"There."

"I don't understand. Why would the newspaper write about Isaac if he was still alive?"

Rebecca looked up, set back in her chair, and struggled to smile.

"He's been wounded, Lucas. Someplace called Cold Harbor."

"Does that mean he's coming home?"

"I don't know. I just don't know."

Rebecca, still mourning the loss of her mother, sat back in her chair. Her head refused to consider the possibility that Isaac might come home. But her heart screamed otherwise. Soldiers survive their wounds all the time, she thought. Isaac, young and healthy, could do the same. She scanned the kitchen for baby Isaac, remembering that Mrs. Burns, the boy's substitute grandmother, took charge of the toddler for the day.

"I'm going to get baby Isaac."

Rebecca reached for her shawl, although it was well into the month of June, for protection against the early, evening breeze. She took the newspaper with her.

"Momma."

Little Isaac, mastering the first word in his vocabulary, made Rebecca's heart leap with joy, each time he uttered her new name. As she scooped the little boy into her arms, Rebecca handed the paper to Mrs. Burns.

"Page two. Isaac was wounded. Where is Cold Harbor?"

Mrs. Burns, slowly reading the list of killed, wounded, and missing in action, recalled that time when Isaac Wells determined that her son, Matt, was safe.

"Cold Harbor is in Virginia, a terrible battle, thousands killed and wounded," said Mrs. Burns, as she pored over the newsprint.

Rebecca, holding baby Isaac tight, sat in the kitchen chair, struggling with her emotions and vowing not to cry.

"He's coming home, Miss Rebecca, I'm sure of it."

"How do you know?"

"My Matthew is watching over him."

Chapter 35

Homeward Bound

"They cost a hundred and fifty dollars."

Isaac, able to rest for a day after his arduous journey from Cold Harbor, lay in a Washington hospital, as their newest patient. The doctor, doing a brisk business in prosthetic devices, explained how the contraption worked. Three leather straps that looped around the thigh securely fastened the carved wooden leg. A moveable foot and a padded opening into which the amputee inserted his stump made the device usable and comfortable.

"I don't have that kind of money," said Isaac, looking away from the unsightly tangle of wood, leather, and buckles.

The doctor, young for his profession, with jet black hair, a mustache, and a sterling white coat, persisted.

"The federal government allocates seventy-five bucks for an artificial leg, fifty for an arm."

"I still don't have that kind of money."

The doctor shrugged.

"You can have this one for seventy-five."

"I don't need your sympathy or your charity. Go away."

"The soldier that owned it died from the fever. You look healthy. It's yours if you want it."

The doctor threw the artificial leg on to Isaac's cot and walked away. His abrupt departure startled Isaac, but the disgruntled soldier did not respond. For more than an hour, Isaac refused to touch the artificial leg, the very sight of it making him angry and bitter. Instead, he glared at the lifeless object and then argued with it.

"It wouldn't work, anyway," he thought. And a while later, "It's probably going to hurt like hell."

Isaac pulled himself into a sitting position and gave the device his dirtiest look. "Well, maybe I'll get lucky and drop dead like the last guy."

Isaac shimmied to the side of the cot, his stump hanging over the edge, as he reached for the device. It weighed more than he thought, the hardwood being of some grain he did not recognize. Although bulky, a pair of boots and a good pair of trousers, made the device invisible. Isaac glanced at the two crutches given him when he first arrived. He hated them more than the artificial limb. The contraption, easier to attach than he imagined, pinched his still tender stump, but Isaac buckled the three leather straps as snugly as he could. Still sitting, he swung the device up and down waving his stump like a broken wing. Except when the heel of his wooden foot hit the hardwood floor, the artificial leg was almost noiseless. Feeling adventurous but surveying his surroundings to ensure that no one was looking, he tried to stand. His forward momentum caused a loss of balance, and he tumbled headlong onto a nearby cot. The occupant, sleeping soundly, reacted poorly.

"What are you doing, Soldier?"

The irate man yanked the blanket to his neck and turned on his side, facing away from Isaac. Where his exposed feet and legs should have been, there was nothing. Isaac scurried to his own cot, his eyes wide and focused on the double amputee's stumps. On his second attempt, Isaac used the crutches, gingerly placing weight on his new foot. He took a few halting steps and with growing confidence a few more.

"That's very good for your first attempt."

Isaac turned quickly, struggling to keep his balance. The

doctor-salesman grinned at his newest customer. Isaac refused to smile, shook his head, and grumbled.

"Better than no leg at all, I guess."

"Walk as much as you can. The further you go, the better you get. Just keep an eye on the stump. Redness, swelling, or an open wound, that's bad. And keep it clean."

Isaac nodded his acknowledgment but remained irritated that the doctor spied on his patient.

Isaac limped down the aisle and headed out the door.

Rebecca surveyed the piles of belongings in her mother's boarding house.

It took weeks to decide what should be sold, what should be moved to the farmhouse, and what should be thrown out. The last room to be emptied, by Rebecca's choice, would be the most difficult, her mother's bedchamber. Some costume jewelry, threadbare dresses, a few baby things from her childhood, and a whole drawer of aprons, forced Rebecca onto a roller coaster of emotions for most of the day. The drawer in her mother's nightstand contained a well-worn Bible, some reading spectacles, and an embroidered handkerchief. She opened the Bible her mother often brought to church services and discovered an unopened letter addressed to Isaac. The handwriting on the envelope told Rebecca that a female, other than her mother, wrote the letter.

For a moment, she considered the unexpressed wishes of its intended recipient, but a burning curiosity overwhelmed her sense of propriety. She opened the letter, read it, and calmly returned the missive to its envelope. Baby Isaac's paternity was not a secret. Nor did Fiona's written expression of love for Isaac surprise or upset the young wife. She wondered if their affair continued after her marriage to Isaac, recalling Isaac's heated denial on the day of his departure. She trusted Isaac to tell the truth.

But she wondered most if Isaac knew that he fathered a son.

Isaac remained in the Washington hospital for weeks.

He walked constantly and became adept at using the prosthetic device, even though the shoe that best fit the wooden foot was a size larger than his other foot. When he wore a pair of baggy trousers, a casual observer could not know that Isaac used a fake leg, a slight hitch in his gait being the only evidence.

Isaac, now eligible to muster out on disability, refused to go home, uncertain if Rebeca, or even the farm, would be there when he returned. The doctor, who Isaac still regarded with suspicion, hovered close and seemed able to read Isaac's thoughts.

"Have you considered the Invalid Corps?"

The young surgeon, clearly knowledgeable on the subject of amputees, explained, "We're up to two battalions, almost all amputees. Some of them fight. Most of them carry weapons, serve as cooks, nurses, or prison guards."

"I've heard of them. They're called the 'cripple brigade'," said Isaac.

"All that's changed. They are officially known as the Veterans Reserve Corps and no more baby blue uniforms. You get to wear the same uniform as every other soldier."

Isaac clung to his misconceptions about the 'cripple brigade,' but agreed to visit the 10th US Reserve Corps, as they were headquartered in Washington. Isaac learned that the special brigade paid a reduced bonus for re-enlisting. And, in his conversations with some of the men in the 10th US Reserve Corps, he realized that the stigma of serving with such a group remained stronger than ever. 'IC' may be the initials for Invalid Corps, but it also designated arms, ammunition, and foodstuffs that were 'inspected and condemned.' Isaac, painfully aware of his defect, did not require the Union army to tell him so.

Isaac's hospital, on the outskirts of the city, lay three miles from the White House. On several occasions, he watched, as a carriage escorted by a handful of soldiers, made its way to the Soldiers Home. The man in the carriage, often wearing a gray shawl and a black stove-pipe top-hat, maintained a suite of rooms at the Soldiers Home, where he often spent the night. On occasion, Abraham Lincoln also dined with the hundreds of soldiers who bivouacked at the same location.

On this day in August, Isaac walked the streets later than usual, it being almost eleven in the evening. The gentle clip-clop of a rider coming in his direction forced the boy to seek cover in some nearby bushes. Isaac no longer trusted his fellow man to be friendly, and he felt no desire to socialize with a stranger. As the rider got closer, a long, lanky frame, the stovepipe top hat, and a gray shawl told Isaac that his commander-in-chief intended to spend the evening at the Soldier's Home. That the president would be unescorted, did not surprise Isaac. Too many people knew that Lincoln often evaded his security detail and preferred to be alone on the streets of Washington.

Even in the moonlight, the old man looked older and more tired than the last time Isaac saw him up-close. Isaac's feelings toward the president also changed, and for the worse. He grew to despise the president, blaming him for the war that never ended and questioning how any man could so blithely ignore the horrible plight of Union soldiers in Confederate prisons. Isaac, within yards of Lincoln, would not miss his intended target, if he had a rifle or even his Colt revolver. And there would be some justice in the assassination of the president, thought Isaac, the man who caused so much loss of life and limb, himself paying the ultimate price.

As the president rode by, a shot rang out. Lincoln's hat flew off, his horse bucked, and the horse took off at a gallop, its rider, leaning backward and bouncing wildly. Isaac looked twice to confirm that his missing gun did not accidentally fire and took only a moment to realize the implications of what just happened. He hesitated, looking both ways to ensure that the president's intended assassin no longer lurked in the area, and left the scene, hopping and walking as fast as he could.

As he approached the hospital, a dozen mounted soldiers rode in his direction. Their leader, a lieutenant, pulled his horse to a sudden stop, forcing the men behind him to do the same.

"Where's your gun?" he barked.

Isaac stood, his arms outstretched, the palms of his hands facing the lieutenant.

"I don't have a gun; they took it away."

"You in some kinda trouble, Boy?"

Isaac lowered his hands and tugged on his pants leg. The lieutenant drew his sidearm and pulled back the hammer.

"Easy, Boy."

Isaac hesitated but continued to roll up his pant leg. By now, he was fuming.

"Is that trouble enough?"

His amputated leg now visible, the lieutenant holstered his weapon.

"Sorry, sir, we're looking for a man with a gun."

"Keep looking."

Isaac turned and hobbled away.

Isaac tossed and turned in his cot, unable to rest.

The lieutenant's interrogation, irritating enough, forced Isaac to consider his true feelings. He lusted for the assassination of Abraham Lincoln, President of the United States. If he possessed a gun, he might well have done it, as easily and as thoughtlessly as he killed so many rebel soldiers. The innocent farm boy, once incapable of killing anyone, wanted to kill everyone. Where Isaac once walked, a monster now marched. Anger and bitterness consumed the boy from Keeseville, no longer a Christian gentleman, no longer a loving husband, son, and brother.

"You hung around here long enough, Wells."

The young doctor, although smiling, explained to his troubled patient that a choice must be made–either a medical discharge or re-enlist. Isaac pulled at his hair, his eyes filled with tears and he stared at the floor. After a moment, Isaac looked up.

"I've done enough killing, Doc. But I can't go home."

Isaac and the doctor filed the necessary paperwork for a medical discharge. With his muster-out wages, he could travel to any city on the East Coast. His thoughts drifted to Albany, a city of pleasant memories and magnificent dreams. As the scenery from his window in the train shifted from tobacco fields to corn fields, Isaac's thinking became clear. Like the leaves on the trees that rushed by his view of the Catskill Mountains, he too underwent a significant change, a change that made his return to Keeseville, the family farm, and Rebecca, impossible. He would return to his hometown just long enough to sell the family farm and then leave for Albany. Once there, he could find work, go to law school part-time, and begin anew the life of an ex-soldier, crippled by war and handicapped by its memories. A broken man cannot expect to heal unless he risks the unknown cures of a new life. The cries of love and the call of war drove Isaac from his home, but his desire for peace and tranquility would be the foundation of his new home. It begins today, Isaac thought.

Chapter 36

All My Love

Isaac could not recall his arrival in Albany or the steamboat ride to Plattsburgh.

The stagecoach bought him to the Wells' family farm, but there was no one to greet him. He walked up the drive, as he did so many times before, the old mare acknowledging his presence with a loud whinny.

He climbed the porch where his father once sat and silently opened the door to the kitchen he had known since childhood. The house was spotless, the Victorian sofa, clean and recovered, looked better than it did when he left several years ago. The buck stove in the kitchen, like the farmhouse, stood cold and empty on this September day. He walked to the bedroom where his honeymoon never happened and sat on the edge of the bed that he would never again share. The old money box was on the maple dresser, stuffed with papers, a bit of currency, and years of memories. As he rifled through the papers, Isaac discovered a letter, addressed to him and opened. The handwriting, unfamiliar but clearly a woman's, prompted him to open the envelope.

My dearest Isaac

I do not expect that you will respond to this letter, but my heart and soul obligate me to write those words which time and circumstances did not permit me to speak. We have known each other for so short a period of time, and I dare not imagine that my life will continue with you at my side. I will, therefore, be content with the knowledge that for a single evening you were my true love and the evidence of that special night will soon be cradled in my arms.

With all my love, Fiona.

Isaac rushed from the house, saddled the old mare, and galloped the horse for the entire trip to Keeseville. He stormed into the Ausable House and accosted the Negro servant. The black man trembled with fear, his mad visitor wild-eyed, with a full beard, mustache, and unkempt hair down to his shoulders.

"Where's Fiona?"

The black man shook his head as if Isaac was speaking a foreign language. Isaac grabbed him by the shirt and pulled him closer.

"I said, where's Fiona? Talk to me, Boy."

"Miss Fiona ain't been here for a while"

"Where is she?"

"Miss Fiona is dead."

Isaac released the man, brushed some imaginary dirt from the servant's clean, white shirt, struggling to compose himself.

"What about the baby. There was a baby."

"I don't know about no baby child," said the servant."

Isaac walked back to his horse and rode aimlessly through the village. He saw the old schoolhouse where Mr. Putnam had beaten John to a bloody pulp. He quickened his pace as he approached Mrs. Lobdell's boarding house. But then he noticed the windows and doors were boarded up; the porch now stripped bare and empty of its rocking chairs. He rode past the Methodist Church where he got married and paused when he reached Sample's Tavern, now under new management and with a new name. No one on the street said hello to the disabled veteran, some of the women crossing the street when he approached. Isaac continued to ride the old mare, the animal now in charge of their destination, its rider too tired and too numb to care. After hours of riding, the pain in Isaac's knee prompted him to pull the horse to a stop. Removing the prosthetic and soaking his stump in cold water made the pain go away. Isaac looked up in search of a river or stream and smiled to himself when he realized that the old mare had brought his master back to the farm. Isaac tugged on the mare's reins and guided the horse through the trees and to the stream where he and John, frolicked as children. He plunged his stump into the cool water, laid back, and settled back for a quiet rest. Isaac could hear the sound of an approaching wagon and several voices. He mounted the old mare, swinging his stump over the saddle, and hooking his fake leg to the horn. He pulled the mare to a halt and dismounted, as the farmhouse came into view. Although across the road, he could see Rebecca with a man and a small child. They were laughing and talking, enjoying a drink, cider thought Isaac.

He studied the young family from his hidden vantage point behind the trees and bushes which lined the road to Port Kent. Rebecca looked happy, he thought. She neither needed nor wanted Isaac in her life anymore. Isaac decided it was time to leave and turned his horse toward the creek, there being two ways to reach the road south.

"Who's out there?"

Rebecca, now standing with one hand on the porch railing, the other shading her view of the road, stared in Isaac's direction.

"I said, who's there?"

The old mare knew Rebecca's voice and bolted for the farmhouse. Isaac grabbed a nearby sapling for balance and watched helplessly as his horse trotted off, with the prosthetic device swinging wildly from the old mare's saddle. The man on the porch scurried into the house and returned with a shotgun.

"Show yourself, or I start shooting."

Isaac hopped closer to the road, secretly hoping that the man with the shotgun would cross the road and fire into the bushes. He just didn't care anymore. Instead, Isaac made himself visible, stopping long enough to retrieve a dead tree branch that served as a makeshift crutch. He struggled to the porch, concentrating on his balance more than the shotgun.

"That's far enough," said the man.

Rebecca studied the stranger. Dirty blond hair fell to his shoulders, a mustache and scraggly beard covered a slightly crooked mouth, and he seemed to favor his left arm, constantly rubbing it with his right hand. But his eyes startled her, a piercing blue color that looked familiar.

"You steal a horse in these parts, and you go to jail," said Lucas.

"I didn't steal your horse."

"Oh, you were intending to return it."

"I stole my horse."

Rebecca used both hands to stifle a scream. She knew those eyes; she fell in love with those eyes.

"My dear, sweet husband has come home."

She flew off the porch and rushed to his side, Isaac struggling to keep his balance as the woman hugged him and kissed his cheek

"Isaac, is that really you?" she asked.

Isaac, stiff and unsmiling, stared at the shotgun, still pointed in his direction.

"Lucas, put that thing away. Now," said Rebecca.

Isaac experienced an epiphany of his own.

"You're the hired hand."

"Your brother hired Lucas, just before you went off to war," said Rebecca.

"And the baby?"

Rebecca focused on Isaac, reaching for his shoulders, and pulling him close.

"That's my baby, and he is the most precious gift I have ever received."

Isaac glared at Lucas and refused to look Rebecca in the eye. He focused on the child.

"What's your baby's name?"

"He's named after his father," said Rebecca.

"Isaac Wells."

Much of the tension in Isaac's mind dissipated when he realized that Rebecca not only waited for his return but also accepted Fiona's child as her own.

The soldier's homecoming celebration began with a bath, a haircut, and a razor. He insisted on the mustache as cover for his crooked mouth and Rebecca insisted on a massive feast. As the hired hands, the neighbors, Mrs. Burns and others filed in and the aroma of chicken with dumplings, filled their home, Rebecca asked Isaac for some private time in their bedchamber. She informed Isaac of her mother's untimely death and John's violent ending. She also gave her husband a detailed report on the financial success of the Wells Family Farms, both of them. Isaac overwhelmed with her tale of woe and wealth, listened but said nothing.

"I missed you so much, Isaac."

"I'm not the man you married, Rebecca."

"I'm not the little girl you married."

"For almost three years, I have done nothing but kill people. And now, I am crippled, the Lord's way of punishing me. I am a one-legged monster, Rebecca, and I don't belong here."

"This is your home, you are my husband, and I will not tolerate such talk, in the future. Do you understand?"

Isaac said nothing, following his wife to the dinner table, without objection.

Isaac lingered over the kitchen chores, while Rebecca put the little boy in his bed. The house, now empty of its company, no longer reverberated with the laughter and loud conversations of friends and family. The eerie silence heightened Isaac's anxiety regarding the marital bedchamber. Not unlike his first encounter with the enemy, the boy decided to run. He slipped into the spare bedroom and removed his fake leg, careful to make no noise, and then donned his nightshirt. When Rebecca appeared at the door, he sat on the edge of his bed, the stump hidden but nothing where his leg used to be.

"I didn't want to interfere with your sleep, he said.

"Have the years since our marriage been unkind to me?"

"No, you are still the most beautiful woman I have ever met."

"I wish to share a bed with my husband."

"I can't, Rebecca, I can't."

Rebecca's eyes filled with tears as she turned away and shut the door behind her.

Isaac and Rebecca continued to live like brother and sister.

Rebecca's entreaties, ignored or repulsed, exacerbated their anxiety. She grew angrier because of the constant rejection, and Isaac responded by withdrawing, feeling useless, unworthy, and defective.

As she gathered eggs from the enclosure which housed their chickens, Rebecca kept a watchful eye on baby Isaac, now running to catch a butterfly. Her husband emerged from the barn, thoughtfully bringing with him a basket, for the dozen or so eggs, now tucked precariously into Rebecca's apron. As he approached, Rebecca screamed. The boy had managed to crawl under the lowest railing of the split log fence which surrounded the pasture. The bull's pasture. The fast-moving toddler angered the beast, who now pawed the dirt and lowered his horns.

Isaac could not run with his fake leg, he tried it and lost his balance, several times. On that particular morning, it didn't seem to matter. Isaac could see only one thing, a little boy chasing an elusive butterfly, while a monstrous bull prepared to charge. The soldier with one leg flew head first under the fence, scrambled to his feet, and yanked the boy, from the monster's path. Isaac turned his back to the bull, sheltering the boy in front of him. The bull charged again, father and son, purposely still. A single horn stabbed into Isaac's wooden leg, tearing the man's pant leg and ripping the device from his thigh. The bull, now struggling with a wood and leather contraption hooked securely onto one of its horns, ran wildly in the opposite direction, the fake leg whipping it into a fury. Isaac hopped his way to the roadside fence and placed the child in Rebecca's outstretched arms.

She held the boy until he fell asleep. As they tucked the child into his bed, each of them kissed the baby's forehead and whispered their love.

As Isaac undressed, she appeared at his door, once more.

"You must never think that your presence here is unnecessary. I need you at my side, Isaac. I love you, and I will always love you."

She turned away; he reached for her hand. They kissed. He struggled with her nightgown. She pulled it over her head and tossed it on the floor.

CPSIA information can be obtained
at www.ICGtesting.com
Printed in the USA
FFHW02n2025221018
48909657-53160FF